THE LIEDER OF BRAHMS

The Lieder of Brahms

MAX HARRISON

PRAEGER PUBLISHERS
New York · Washington

BOOKS THAT MATTER

Published in the United States of America in 1972
by Praeger Publishers, Inc., 111 Fourth Avenue,
New York, N.Y. 10003

© 1972 by Max Harrison

Library of Congress Catalog Card Number: 79–165847

Printed in Great Britain

Contents

For Alison

In some of its more complex and most characteristic forms of expression, music seems to have established itself later than the other arts. True, Gothic architecture had a parallel in the contrapuntal richness of the so-called Netherlands School, but more usual was the case of religious painting of the early Italian Renaissance, which lacked a worthy musical counterpart until the days of Palestrina. Such correspondences did grow more common, however, and the time-lag shorter. Some later aspects of secular Renaissance painting and poetry, for example, were reflected by English and Italian madrigals and in lute songs from Spain, France and, again, Italy and England; Protestantism found its musical voice in Germany with Heinrich Schütz and J. S. Bach.

To begin with, German developments were even slower than in these other countries, and little of significance appears to have occurred before about the middle of the fifteenth century—by which time, for example, the first great period of French music was nearly over. Yet once under way, the German tradition asserted a quite singular character, and maintained a continuity which was very much a consequence of that character.

This is best appreciated if we come nearer to our own time and contrast subsequent German music with that of other countries. The training of a composer such as Brahms, like that of earlier and even considerably later German musicians, was based on a consideration of J. S. Bach and his successors, with little attention given to earlier works or to those from other countries. Harmonic and contrapuntal study, for instance, depended on Fux, not on Palestrina or his Flemish antecedents, and C. P. E. Bach could say 'The fundamentals of my father's art and my own are anti-Rameau'. As we shall see, Brahms himself moved, in a very limited way and like a few of his fellow German composers, against this sort of exclusiveness, which had no artistic parallel elsewhere in Europe during his time. He soon developed an enthusiasm for sixteenth-century music that was duly echoed in some of his output—in the austere harmonies of *Die Trauernde* Op. 7 no. 5, for example, or his madrigal-like *All' meine Herzgedanken* Op. 62 no. 5, a *Lied* and a part-song respectively. Other signs of his unobtrusive independence can be found, such as the motet *Wenn wir in höchsten Nöten sind* Op. 110 no. 3, where he completely ignores the major-keyed tune used by J. S. Bach and employs a considerably more angular line in the minor. However, even such works still were very much conditioned by the long-established precepts of German tradition, which, admittedly, often gave rise to music of rare and subtle complexity that was essentially dialectical in method. Each composer built directly on the technical procedures of his predecessors and perhaps on those of his contemporaries. Thus Haydn and Mozart learnt from each other, thus the once seemingly divergent tendencies of Wagner and Brahms came together in Schoenberg—this latter being a reconciliation more than adequately signposted, as we shall see, in a number of Brahms's own works.

The idealized sensuality of some Brahms *Lieder* might have an apparent counterpart within the French tradition in certain Fauré songs, but, even if his sympathies were a little wider than is normally supposed, German practice left no room for real eclecticism. The allegedly oriental accents of Brahms's *Geliebter, wo zaudert dein irrender Fuss* Op. 33 no. 13 are wholly unconvincing, while his settings of Daumer's Hafiz translations—*Bitteres zu sagen denkst du* Op. 32 no. 7, *Botschaft* and *Liebesglut* Op. 47 nos. 1 and 2, for example—are similarly without authenticity—a poor response, on the part both of composer and translator, to Persia's great poet, especially when compared with the *Hafiz Liebeslieder* Opp. 24 and 26 by Szymanowski (which use Bethge's superior German translations). An earlier German setting of Hafiz, Weber's *Rosen im Haare* Op. 66 no. 2 (in Breuer's translation) is no better. The nearest Brahms ever got to the required idiom was in the melismata of the Adagio to his Clarinet Quintet Op. 115, although there is a fleeting hint of the style in the second half of the first of his Sarabandes for piano, published posthumously in 1927.

In contrast, the teaching of Dukas or d'Indy shows that the attractions of experiment, of new idioms and of the exotic, were felt in France even by academics. A few earlier composers such as Couperin had expressed and almost codified a wide range of human emotions in terms of a deliberately narrow stylistic range, but the French were usually open to new sensations and to fresh modes of expression. Debussy's concern with Balinese music or Roussel's employment of genuine Indian resources in his opera-ballet *Padmâvatî* both testify to this. For a more specific instance of these different attitudes one might compare, say, uses of the whole-tone scale (pioneered by Dargomijsky, Glinka and, of course, Liszt, although known to earlier theorists) in German and French works.

The form of Schoenberg's Chamber Symphony No. 1 Op. 9 is greatly influenced by the partly whole-tone outline of its main theme. However, development of these whole-tone factors is conditioned by the underlying functional tensions of the harmony which unite the entire piece and this despite many passages being conceived in primarily contrapuntal terms. Further, these whole-tone elements are combined with other quite different harmonic entities, such as chords built on fourths, that are likewise fitted into, and affected by, the over-all form. In contrast with this careful relating of a new resource to established procedures, Debussy writes many passages that melodically and harmonically are made almost exclusively from whole-tone elements; his approach to harmony is essentially vertical, taking the quality or character of his chords' specific sound as the basis for structural unity and liberating them from the necessity of harmonic argument.

As implied, the continuity of German traditions did not begin with J. S. Bach; a number of basic elements or tendencies survived from much earlier, surfacing, chiefly in song, when music and literature came into a favourable relationship. This is shown clearly enough in Brahms *Lieder* such as *Ich schell mein Horn ins Jammertal* Op. 43 no. 3, which decidedly echoes the sixteenth century. Note how a full opening bar is given to '*Ich*', just as in Arnt von Aich's 1519 setting of the same words. It is instructive to compare the two melodies as a whole.

Naturally, Brahms's harmonization underlines his melody's archaic aspect, partly by avoiding sevenths. Similar cases are *Die Trauernde* Op. 7 no. 5, which has only two sevenths, and *Vom verwundeten Knaben* Op. 14 no. 2, which has but a few. The simplicity of the accompaniment to *Ein Sonett* Op. 14 no. 4 produces a comparable effect, and the parallel fifths of *Vom verwundeten Knaben* should be noted. *Ein Sonett* uses Herder's translation of verses by Thibault, Count of Champagne, King of Navarre. Although in this case the difference of character is far greater, the style of old French songs differing considerably from that of old German songs, it is again interesting to set the ancient melody, also by Thibault, beside that of Brahms, which again has some of the aspects of a genuine *Minnelied*. The former is shown with the version of the text which appeared in the *Chansons Choisies* anthology published at Paris in 1765.

4

Thibault

Las! si j'a - vais pouvoir d'oubli - er sa beau-té, sa beauté, son bien di-re, et son très doux, très doux regar-der, fi-ni-rois mon marty - - re, mais las! mon cœur je n'en puis ô-ter, et grand affo - la-ge m'est dés-pé - rer - mais tel ser - vage donne cou-rage à tout en-du - rer - Et puis com-ment, comment oubli - er sa beau-té, sa beauté, son bien di-re, et son très doux, très doux regarder? Mieux aime mon marty - - re.

Langsam, sehr innig

Brahms Op.14 no.4 (1858)

Ach Könnt ich, könn-te ver - ges-sen sie, ihr schö-nes, lie-bes, lieb-liches We-sen, den Blick, die freundli-che Lip - pe die! Viel-leicht ich möchte ge-

poco più animato

ne-sen! Doch ach, mein Herz, mein Herz kann es nie! Und doch ist's Wahnsinn zu hof-fen sie! Und um sie schweben gibt Mut und Le-ben, zu wei-chen nie - - . . . etc.

The words of *Hüt du dich* Op. 66 no. 5 are also very old, having appeared in Berg and Newber's *68 Lieder* printed at Nuremberg in 1542; likewise those of *Vor der Tür* Op. 28 no. 2, for Hoffmann von Fallersleben's 1844 poem is based on verses that appeared in Forster's *Der Ander theil Kurtzweiliger guter frischer Teutscher Liedlein zu singen vast lustig*, published at Nuremberg in 1540.

Sometimes, however, Brahms chose comparatively modern texts that looked back far into the past, such as the poems from Tieck's *Wunderschöne Liebesgeschichte der schönen Magelone und des Grafen Peter aus der Provence* of 1797, which provided fifteen episodes of knightly adventure for his Op. 33 cycle.

5

Entführung Op. 97 no. 3, its chain-mailed kidnapper making off across the moors with Lady Judith, speaks of a similar world, as do the characters of *Die Nonne und der Ritter* Op. 28 no. 1. *Das Lied vom Herrn von Falkenstein* Op. 43 no. 4 describes a feudal situation, and Op. 71 no. 5 is actually called *Minnelied*. The origins of several nineteenth-century German operatic librettos form another link with the remote past; the minne-singer Wolfram von Eschenback's version of *Parsifal* and Godfrey of Strasbourg's version of *Tristan* were Wagner's starting points; the original source of the libretto for Weber's *Euryanthe* (a score that evokes the world of medieval chivalry besides containing remarkable anticipations of Wagner, and not just of *Lohengrin*) was the thirteenth-century *Roman de la violette* by Gilbert de Montreuil. Similar links with a distant musical past can also be found in nineteenth-century German instrumental works, and the Andante of Brahms's Piano Sonata No. 2 Op. 2 includes free variations on an old melody by Kraft von Toggenburg. However, as we shall see later, composers, especially in Germany, had considerable difficulty in reconciling old material of this sort, including folk songs both genuine and spurious, with their modern techniques.

Because of what was said above on the tendency of German musical practice to diverge in important respects from that of other countries, it is interesting to note that the German minnesingers derived from the French troubadours and trouvères. From around 1100, these latter had a great effect on poetry throughout Europe, influencing both Dante and Chaucer, and they refined poetic and musical procedures and the relation between the two arts. Trouvère and troubadour poetry employed about 900 different metres and forms of stanza, and they especially developed the lyrical aspects of both verse and melody. Although they too were aristocratic poet-musicians like the French, German minnesingers, who began somewhat later and flourished mainly in the twelfth to fourteenth centuries, also took love, nature, heroism and religion as their subjects. But unlike the troubadours and trouvères they did not celebrate national pride or take sides in political disputes, and this less public, more domestic, emphasis was prophetic, like their assimilation of folk music, of several aspects of much later German song. Nor were their verse metres so numerous or so complex.

6

Subject matter was still further limited and many restrictive, pedantic rules were applied by the craftsmen and traders of the mastersinger literary and musical cult in the fourteenth to sixteenth centuries. This began at Mainz shortly before 1323 when an academic attempt was made in Toulouse to preserve troubadour art. Henry of Meissen, last of the minnesingers and the first mastersinger, founded the Mainz guild in 1311. Many others followed all over Germany and a few were still active in the seventeenth century, the last one, at Ulm, being dissolved early in Brahms's lifetime, during 1839 (its last member dying in 1876). Of course, the more remote days of this movement are portrayed with considerable accuracy in Wagner's opera *Die Meistersinger von Nürnberg*, and some of their music looks forward, however distantly, to such things as the domestic religious songs of C. P. E. Bach and to other direct antecedents of the nineteenth-century *Lied*. It is still often said that the *Lied* was a result of changes in late eighteenth-century literature, but these links with distant times show the persistence of tendencies in German music which are themselves enough to suggest that the *Lied* was not just a consequence of recent literature any more than it was spontaneously invented by Schubert. That it is simply another realization of specific aspects of the German tradition is further emphasized by the fact that the mastersingers, and the minnesingers still more, thought of themselves as poets as much as musicians, so their work hints at the *Gesamtkunstwerk** ideal that was of such importance to nineteenth-century artists. But there were other reasons, not all of them musical, for the sympathy towards—if not always understanding of—the distant past shown in the music of Brahms and other German composers of his time.

It is quite true, of course, that literature and music did often reflect one another during the nineteenth century, yet each followed its own independent lines of development. German Romantic writers sought to express thoughts and feelings which the eighteenth century—the Age of Enlightenment, or *Aufklärung*—had bypassed, even though this movement itself had only been a reaction against the dominance of religion in

---

* The *Gesamtkunstwerk* was a work which attempted to combine all the arts.

seventeenth-century German intellectual life; theoretical bases of the earliest Romantics' activities were laid by the Schlegel brothers and in such works as Wackenroder's *Herzensergiessungen eines kunstliebenden Klosterbruders* of 1797. Tieck, already mentioned with regard to Brahms's *Magelone Romanzen* Op. 33, was associated with the first Romantic school of writers, founded at Jena (which, appropriately enough, is close to Weimar) in 1798, and though his later short stories have greater value, his early writings—fantastic comedies and novels, macabre fairy tales and plays—illustrate the reaching for new horizons. Similarly, Novalis (Friedrich von Hardenberg), admired by Weber, produced lyrics and fragmentary novels that, juxtaposing romantic medievalism and Christian mysticism, took his readers into the world of the *Märchen* and represented a considerable imaginative achievement, especially in *Heinrich von Ofterdingen* (1802). Jean Paul Richter, a disciple of Herder, also wrote somewhat formless novels, such as *Die Flegeljahre* which provided a starting point for Schumann's *Papillons* Op. 2, but their sentiment and lavish detail won them popularity.

Such writers sought a relief from the dullness, as they felt it, of their own day in the literature and general culture of the Middle Ages, with its supposedly chivalrous and romantic aspirations, its gracious ladies, gallant knights and pious monks. (Some of the Pre-Raphaelite paintings show the same tendency in a later generation.) Essentially their longing was not for the past, about which, initially, they had little exact knowledge, but rather for what Delius much later called 'The wide, far distance', for something unattainable, for dreams, emotions, visions as an end in themselves. This survived in Romantic music right down to such very late pieces as Mahler's 1902 Rückert setting, *Ich bin der Welt abhanden gekommen*—a reverie during which time almost stands still; and of course music, with its intangible character, was always better suited to such moods and aspirations than books or pictures, for as E. T. A. Hoffmann, one of Schumann's heroes, said, it was '*The* Romantic art'.

Certainly these aspirations run through much nineteenth-century music, down to the elegiac, consolatory Intermezzos of Brahms's piano cycles Opp. 116–19 and beyond. They are embodied many times in his *Lieder*, in youthful celebrations of natural beauty like *Juchhe!* Op. 6 no. 4 (its excessive word-repetitions notwithstanding), in the twilight nostalgia of *Abenddämmerung* Op. 49 no. 5, in the dreamlike and highly characteristic *Vorüber* Op. 58 no. 7 or *Meine Lieder* Op. 106 no. 4. Less typical of Brahms yet in common with the early Romantics is the supernatural evocation of *Steig auf, geliebter Schatten* Op. 94 no. 2 (though what is perhaps an unconscious echo of that influence is the violin passage in the development section of the opening Allegro to his Symphony No. 2 Op. 73, reminiscent of Mendelssohn's *Erste Walpurgisnacht* overture Op. 60). And before this, when the literary Romantic Movement was beginning, music hinted at its coming emphases in the *Affektenlehre* doctrine of Quantz and C. P. E. Bach, which held that the chief purpose of music was to portray specific emotions. Although rather schematic and even a bit rationalistic, this was an advance, in expressive terms, on the previously dominant Italian *stile galante* and pointed towards Beethoven.

Foreign influences played an important rôle in this widening of horizons; A. W. Schlegel made a number of Shakespeare translations between 1797 and 1810, while Tieck, who collaborated in these, had early developed an enthusiasm not only for Shakespeare but for other Elizabethan dramatists and for Spanish drama. Already, in the eighteenth century, imitations and translations of the English *Guardian, Tatler* and *Spectator* had appeared—the *Moralische Wochenschriften* as they were called—and in general English, and particularly Scots, literature were among several strong influences.

Besides his settings of Ophelia's songs from *Hamlet*, which have no opus number and were only published in 1933 (the centenary of his birth), Brahms made a choral setting of 'Come away, Death' from *Twelfth Night* as *Komm herbei, Tod* Op. 17 no. 2. Also he told his friend Dietrich that Schumann's Op. 25 no. 13 setting of Burns's 'My heart's in the Highlands', in Wilhelm Gerhard's 1840 translation (*Mein Herz ist im Hochland*), inspired the finale of his Piano Sonata No. 1 Op. 1, or at least its A minor episode—though he might also have been unconsciously influenced by the opening movement of Mendelssohn's Symphony No. 3 Op. 56 'The Scottish'. Other Scots literary echoes in Brahms's instrumental works are, of course, his quotation of lines from *Lady Anne Bothwell's Lament*, in Herder's translation, at the head of his keyboard Intermezzo Op. 117 no. 1, and the Ballad Op. 10 no. 1, also for piano, which almost certainly began life as a vocal setting of the Scots ballad *Edward*, again in a translation by Herder. This was finally given a successful vocal setting as Op. 75 no. 1, although Brahms unfortunately chose the version which appeared in Herder's *Volkslieder* of 1779 rather than the more vivid translation from his 1774 *Alte Volkslieder*. There were many other settings of this piece: by Loewe Op. 1 no. 1, Schubert D. 923, and Tchaikovsky Op. 46 no. 2 (in Tolstoy's translation), and in general the influence on Romantic music is underlined by the 'Rob Roy' and 'Waverley' overtures of Berlioz, the Scots operas of Rossini, Marschner and Donizetti, and especially by Boïeldieu's *La Dame Blanche* (based on Sir Walter Scott's *Guy Mannering*), which quotes some actual Scots melodies.

The first Romantic school dispersed in 1804 and was followed in 1806 by a second at Heidelberg, whose most characteristic production was a collection of—largely rewritten—German folk poems called *Des Knaben Wunderhorn*, published in 1806–8, by Achim von Arnim and Clemens Brentano. This cast a very long shadow across German poets and composers, some of the texts being set much later by Mahler, Richard Strauss and others. Brahms made only two solo *Wunderhorn* settings, *Der Überläufer* and *Liebesklage des Mädchens* Op. 48 nos. 2 and 3, but he also used *Hüt du dich* Op. 66 no. 5 and *Guter Rat* Op. 75 no. 2 as duets and made choral settings of *Rosmarin* and *Von alten Liebesliedern* Op. 62 nos. 1 and 2. His *Lieder* also include Brentano's *O kühler Wald* Op. 72 no. 3, his choral works the same poet's *Abendständchen* Op. 42 no. 1 and Arnim's *O süsser Mai* Op. 93a no. 3.

When this school broke up around 1809, it split into two—one group in the north and one associated with Württemberg. Among the former was Prussia's greatest dramatic poet, Heinrich von Kleist, a leading writer in the patriotic movement against Napoleon and at the same time one who believed music to be the root of the other arts. Both on these diverse matters and in his view that the only sure things in life are the unconscious voices of feeling and instinct, Kleist well accords with the earlier Heidelberg poets, who likewise strengthened the national and patriotic spirit and prepared the way for a rising against Napoleon. In politics this union between Romantic ideas and national feeling affected German thought in some ways for the rest of the nineteenth century and helped to differentiate it from other European intellectual traditions in a way analogous to the distinctions between German music and that of other countries noted above.

Altogether the Heidelberg group was more practical than the first gathering of Romantic writers at Jena, and in place of the fantasies of Tieck or Novalis it favoured actual historical work. Perhaps because of this its long-term effect was greater, and to it must be credited the foundation of German philology and the systematic study of German medieval literature. Notable contributors to German medieval scholarship were Lachmann, Wilhelm and Jakob Grimm; the study of texts and sources was later formalized as an academic discipline, under the growing influence of science and technology, by such men as Scherer, Minor and Schmidt.

Quite apart from their unearthing of major figures like Palestrina and J. S. Bach, musicians, like writers of that period, showed a curiosity over the past that would have been rare indeed during previous centuries. Besides the intuitive sympathy with distant times already illustrated in Brahms's *Lieder*, it may be noted that he found the carol *Josef, lieber Josef mein*—used as a *cantus firmus* in *Geistliches Wiegenlied* Op. 91 no. 2—in Corner's *Gross-Katholisches Gesangbuch* of 1631, hardly a book that a song composer of an earlier generation would have sought out. Another sign of this absorption in certain facets of the past is that Brahms only became aware of contemporary music when he was twenty, the study of older works having occupied him exclusively until then. The same was true of Berlioz a generation earlier, for he steeped himself in Gluck and Spontini before coming upon Beethoven and Weber.

Goethe claimed to be the first to use 'Romantic' as a distinction from 'Classical', and certainly he went far beyond the *Aufklärung*'s substitution of science for religion. The Romantic

Movement proper was less a reaction against Weimar classicism than an extension of its interests, particularly its initial emphasis on Greece, which was thought of as a kind of lost paradise. This was stimulated especially by Lessing and Winckelmann, and it was by Lessing's example that German literature made such advances in the second half of the eighteenth century. Evocations of the ancient world can be found in a considerable number of nineteenth-century *Lieder*: Brahms's *Phänomen* Op. 61 no. 3, a duet, and *Der Abend* Op. 64 no. 2, a part-song, among them; these are settings of Goethe and Schiller respectively. Less direct yet very beautiful instances are Mörike's *An eine Äolsharfe* Op. 19 no. 5 and Hölty's *Die Schale der Vergessenheit* Op. 46 no. 3, a song Brahms was at first reluctant to publish. *Die Kränze* Op. 46 no. 1 is another case, its text coming from the *Antike Musen: Hellas* section of Daumer's *Polydora, ein weltpoetisches Liederbuch*, which the author said was intended to make Germans more aware of the poetry of Greece and Rome. This tendency survived into our own century with Hauer's many Hölderlin settings, which carry an echo, not only in the texts, of the early Romantics' longing for Greece.

The popularity of James Macpherson's *Ossian*, poorly translated into German hexameters by Michael Denis in 1768–9, is another sign of the widespread, and sustained, concern with legend. Many Romantic compositions were inspired by this book, including the operas *Oithona* by Barthélemon, Méhul's *Uthal*—whose orchestration probably influenced Brahms to omit violins from his Serenade No. 2 Op. 16 and the first movement of his Requiem Op. 45—and *Ossian* by Lesueur, Berlioz's teacher. There also are nine *Ossian* settings by Schubert and two by Brahms, *Gesang aus Fingal* Op. 17 no. 4 and *Darthulas Grabesgesang* Op. 42 no. 3 (again using a Herder translation), for female and mixed chorus respectively.

Though Schumann in particular had continued to be influenced by Richter, E. T. A. Hoffmann and others, most of this musical activity was not simply a reflection of the ideas of the earliest Romantic writers. The rule of reactionary governments, exemplified later by that of Metternich in Austria, had caused much frustration among intellectuals because they restricted freedom of thought, and it became unlikely that earlier cultural and social ideals would be realized. Some, like

Hölderlin (the great lyric poet and author of a fine novel, *Hyperion*, 1797–9), despaired of their fulfilment; a feeling of disillusionment over man's capability of reaching lofty goals, and a pessimistic view of his place in the universe, marked imaginative literature and clouded the early Romantics' optimism. But there was a renewed seeking-out of fresh avenues following the Napoleonic wars that, along with much else, produced the historical studies noted above. A concern with Teutonic mythology, typified by A. W. Schlegel's enthusiasm for the *Nibelungenlied*, which finally resulted in Wagner's *Der Ring des Nibelungen* and in Hebbel's *Die Nibelungen* trilogy, partly answered his complaint, in *Über dramatische Kunst und Literatur* (1809–11), that 'The greatest deficiency of modern art is that artists have no mythology to fall back on'. It also gave rise to the widespread interest in folklore and folk or quasi-folk music, although this had partially been anticipated in the later eighteenth century by the *Volkstümliche Lieder* of composers belonging to the *Zweite Berliner Liederschule* such as Reichardt, Zelter, J. A. Schultz and others. This, in reaction to the coloratura aria (*Kunstlied*), assumed a mode of folkish expression that if still somewhat artificial was an advance on the affected *naïveté* of earlier attempts in that direction, typified by J. A. Hiller's *Fünfzig geistliche Lieder für Kinder* (1774), although both, perhaps, may be seen as instances of the German tradition neutralizing outside influences.

Romanticism, however, with its insistence on the true value of feeling in the face of the limitations of reason, on the worth of emotion, instinct, fancy, intuition, linked man inevitably with nature and welcomed any form of untutored expression, particularly lyrical expression. (Hence, perhaps, the undis-criminating attitude to folk music adopted by German composers later, especially Brahms.) Because of this, Percy's *Reliques of Ancient English Poetry*—much of the contents of which actually were Scots—enjoyed a Continental popularity comparable to that of Macpherson's *Ossian*, both these books having a considerable effect on Goethe through the influence of Herder. The latter translated both works into German and the text of Brahms's Op. 14 no. 3, *Murrays Ermordung*, is from the *Reliques*, as are those of the pair of *Weg der Liebe* duets Op. 20 nos. 1 and 2.

Another example of this tendency was the wide acceptance

among intellectuals of James Fenimore Cooper's novels portraying the supposedly noble savage in direct communion with unspoilt nature, and his works were read by Schubert, Berlioz and other musicians. Indeed, following both Goethe and J.-J. Rousseau, German Romantic writers such as those already mentioned, together with Rückert, Heine, Uhland, Eichendorff, Lenau, Platen and many others whose names later became familiar to connoisseurs of *Lieder*, frequently expressed emotional responses to nature and to man's relation with it. As usual, Brahms's songs illustrate the German musical tradition's translation of this, not only with mature considerations of natural beauty like *Sommerabend* Op. 85 no. 1, but in pieces such as *Auf dem See* Op. 59 no. 2, *Mondenschein* Op. 85 no. 2 or *Feldeinsamkeit* Op. 86 no. 2, which intimately relate man's emotions to natural phenomena, stressing the unity between them. Though it is possible to single out a group of *Lieder* such as his seven songs Op. 95 which completely avoid natural imagery, the texts of some eighty out of the 198 *Lieder* which Brahms published refer to nature in a way significant to their argument.

The concern with folk song that was an essential complement to this marks countless nineteenth-century works and must be related to the tides of nationalism so prominent both in music and elsewhere. Even to begin with, this was not simply a question of quasi-folk melodies like those of, say, Krufft, who produced a Viennese equivalent to the Berlin *Volkstümliches Lied* noted above—though his songs, with their free keyboard accompaniments and attempts at *durchkomponiert** music, do appear to have influenced Schubert. More significant is the case of Weber, in whose *Der Freischütz* German folk myth gives rise to the contours of German folk song, modifying the basically Italian melodic language. It seems prophetic of the later German *Lied* that this idiom, despite such things as the Huntsmen's Chorus in *Der Freischütz*, is best suited to quiet, introspective or picturesque moods, and it is noticeable in Weber's *Euryanthe*, where folk song again has a considerable influence,

---

* *Durchkomponiert*, meaning literally 'through-composed', is a term used to describe songs in which the music is different for each stanza of the poem.

that the larger, the more grand, the gesture becomes, the less German, the more conventionally Italian, the music is. Of course, such a composer was a creative musician, not a scholar, and authenticity was never a real consideration; this distinction is illustrated by Brahms as clearly as by any of Weber's successors.

Like so many other musicians of that time, Brahms's teacher, Marxsen, responded to the general interest and became concerned with folk song, or something like it. This is shown by his two sets of variations Op. 67, one on an unspecified 'peasant dance', the other on a Finnish folk melody, and also by his *100 Variations on a Folk Song*, published much later, in 1883 at Brahms's expense. Brahms himself reacted similarly, and while his *Volkslied* and *Die Trauernde* Op. 7 nos. 4 and 5 should be noted as his first settings of supposed folk poems, the music of the latter song, as mentioned earlier, reflected his interest in the sixteenth-century choral repertoire. Despite the Italianism of Weber and the vital rôle of his works in the growth of German Romanticism, that country's art music showed its usual powers of resistance to outside influences, even to those of its native folk songs, and often what appeared to be outside influences were, as we shall see, actually nothing of the sort.

Altogether, the *Lieder* of Brahms contain some forty settings of what are described as folk poems, but even the status of these as folk art must be questioned, and later in this book his ambiguous position with regard to authentic folk music is discussed in some detail. Meanwhile, examples may be quoted of the apparent influence of folk song on Brahms's own highly cultivated art, such as *Der Überläufer* and *Vergangen ist mir Glück und Heil* Op. 48 nos. 2 and 6. There is no denying the aeolian modality of the former's melody nor the latter's dorian. Yet, as with the instances given earlier—of the affinities between, say, *Vom verwundeten Knaben* Op. 14 no. 2 or *Ich schell mein Horn ins Jammertal* Op. 43 no. 3 and the songs of the minnesingers—this is as likely to be an unconscious result of the persistence of certain basic tendencies within the German musical tradition as to be a conscious response to the comparatively new concern with folk music. That modality had retained a place in sophisticated German art music—albeit an inconclusive one—independent of folk song is shown, of course, by the *Heiliger Dankgesang* of Beethoven's String Quartet No. 15 Op. 132, which, as the score deliberately points out, is '*in der lydischen Tonart*'. Again, while the accompaniment of *Der Überläufer* is chordally very plain (no dominant seventh, as in *Ich schell mein Horn ins Jammertal*), the bass, in octaves, assumes an independence towards the close of each verse, as if deliberately to lend interest otherwise lacking in the texture. Further, the solo version of *Vergangen ist mir Glück und Heil*, Op. 48 no. 6, should be compared with Brahms's mixed choir setting, Op. 62 no. 7. The effect of the former's dorian melody is softened by major dominants and by minor sixths in the harmonization, while the latter is unequivocally in D minor, with C sharp twice appearing in the melody.

It was principally Wackenroder who discovered the Gothic world for his fellow Romantics and who proclaimed the affinity between music and the essential qualities of German intellectual traditions. Rare cases like Goethe notwithstanding, the German spirit, as preceding comments on the recurring tendencies of German music suggest, is not most happily expressed in poetry because it is at once too abstract and too rationalistic. It is striking that the realistic forms of drama and the novel, so well represented in, say, English literature, arrived, in quantity, comparatively late on the German scene. German thought was better suited to dialectical processes so well illustrated in that country's art music. Not for nothing was so gifted a writer as Hölderlin ashamed of his language, finding it weak in expressive power beside music; nor is it surprising that Tieck could say, in his *Phantasien über die Kunst* (his continuation of Wackenroder's *Herzensergiessungen eines kunstliebenden Klosterbruders*) that 'Without music the earth is like a barren, incomplete house with its dwellers missing'.

Some writers distrusted the effect of music nonetheless, and particularly Goethe. Under Zelter's influence he expressed initial dislike of Beethoven's work, and precisely because of the dominance of music over verse in true Romantic *Lied*, preferred Zelter's plain settings of his poems to those of Schubert; his receipt of a copy of Schubert's *Der Erlkönig* D. 328 was not even acknowledged (just as he ignored Beethoven's cantata *Meeresstille und glückliche Fahrt* Op. 112). One suspects that

Goethe would similarly have placed Reichardt's setting of *Harzreise im Winter* far above Brahms's Alto Rhapsody Op. 53, which uses the same text, just as later Allmers preferred Focken's sentimental treatment of *Feldeinsamkeit* to what he called the 'artificial melody' of Brahms's Op. 86 no. 2.

Despite reservations comparable to those of Goethe—he spoke of a 'constant strumming on the piano'—Schiller often calls for music in his plays, uses musical characterizations and metaphors, and liked to have it played in the next room as he was writing. All this confirms the increased use of music as a literary effect in German writing from about 1770 onwards. Lady Caroline in Klinger's play *Sturm und Drang*, Wackenroder's Josef Berglinger, who heard 'sounds that seem to be words', even Lotte in Goethe's *Werther*, together with other characters, such as those from the novels of Heinse, all lead to Hoffmann's Kreisler in *Die Lebensansichten des Katers Murr*, perhaps the greatest fictional musician.

Writers of the more extravagant verse and prose such as Hoffmann were continually drawn to music (as composers like Schumann were, in turn, drawn to such writers) because its more leisurely expression makes a more determined appeal to the senses than words that must produce their effect via ideas. Hoffmann was able to compare J. S. Bach's motets with the 'daring, wonderful, Romantic' structure of Strasbourg Cathedral, and later Whistler called his paintings 'symphonies and nocturnes—harmonies in tone'. Fusion of the arts was indeed a great Romantic preoccupation, and early in the century Herder had desired such a union, while Hegel even spoke of a *Weltgeist*, a world spirit. The feeling was particularly intense among Germans, and perhaps the *Gesamtkunstwerk* was related to the nineteenth-century political ideal of unification, for even as early as 1812 there had been calls for a united German Reich. Romantic writers, at least, had no doubt that music was to be the basis of the *Gesamtkunstwerk*, Hoffmann, as we have seen, calling it 'The most Romantic of the arts', and Wackenroder 'The art of arts'. Kleist tried to find hidden poetic forms in counterpoint, and maintained that his plays were composed musically, this being a kind of reflection of Schumann's remark 'I learnt more counterpoint from Jean Paul [Richter] than from my music teacher'. Significantly, when he reviewed Hoffmann's *Undine* (1816), Weber described

17

it as 'The kind of opera all Germans want: a self-contained work of art wherein all separate elements contributed by the arts in co-operation dissolve and reappear to create a new world.' Whether the other arts would join in or not, there seemed no doubt that, as the Countess was much later to say in Richard Strauss's *Capriccio*, words and music would be 'fused into a new whole'.

Despite this, solo songs were produced only in small numbers in the immediate pre-Romantic period, at least in comparison with the vast quantities written by Schubert and Wolf, or even by Schumann and Brahms. Until Schubert, the song with piano accompaniment, despite all its links with the distant past, was not considered a primary mode of artistic expression; most of the energy composers had for vocal composition— Mozart's, for example—went into opera or church music. And though Schubert's vital influence on all later German *Lieder* writers, and upon Brahms perhaps more than on any other, cannot be questioned, not all the relevant lines of development passed through him.

Notwithstanding, say, the perfect articulation of Goethe's text, qualified by a symmetrical musical design, in Beethoven's *Wonne der Wehmut* Op. 83 no. 1, this and most of his other songs are descended from Reichardt and other composers of the *Zweite Berliner Liederschule*, rather than being direct precursors of Schubert. In the same way, although a few of his songs, like *Die Liebende schreibt* Op. 86 no. 3, suggest the influence of Schumann, most of Mendelssohn's songs also derive from the Berlin composers (especially his teacher Zelter), rather than from Schubert. More direct are certain anticipations of the nineteenth-century *Lied* to be found in *Singspiel* and opera, and in some instrumental music, such as the extremely romantic slow movements of C. P. E. Bach, who, perhaps significantly, was a friend of Lessing and Klopstock.

In operas like Beethoven's *Fidelio* (originally produced in 1805) or *La Vestale* by Spontini (1807) there is something of the *Lied*'s fusion of recitative and aria, while '*Les dieux prendront pitié*' from the latter work has definite hints of Schubert. The operas of Marschner, a Weber disciple, are usually mentioned because of the way *Der Templer und die Jüdin* and *Hans Heiling* (rather than *Der Vampyr*) anticipate Wagner—specifically *Der fliegende Holländer* and *Lohengrin*. Yet these works prefigure other aspects of later nineteenth-century German music, and in, for example, the second of Wolf's *Michelangelo-Lieder* of 1897, *Alles endet, was entstehet*, an echo of Rebecca's Prayer from *Der Templer* (1829) may be caught. Similarly, the left-hand theme at bar 45 of Brahms's piano Scherzo Op. 4 derives from the *Hans Heiling* overture.

Recitative survives as such, of course, in some *Lieder*, including Brahms's *An eine Äolsharfe* Op. 19 no. 5, the opening of which is actually headed 'Recit.'; similar cases, though not so marked, are his *Mondenschein* Op. 85 no. 2 and *Heimkehr* Op. 7 no. 6. *Auf dem Kirchhofe* Op. 105 no. 4 contrasts recitative and aria elements in a way that is unusually explicit for its late date—about 1888—the latter actually deriving from the chorale '*O Haupt voll Blut und Wunden*'. However, such cases must be heard in relation to the interchange of *arioso* and declamation found in Schubert *Lieder* such as *Gruppe aus dem Tartarus* D. 583 or the Heine settings of his *Schwanengesang* D. 957. Other instances of operatic overtones in Brahms *Lieder* include *Nicht mehr zu dir zu gehen, beschloss ich* Op. 32 no. 2. More direct, perhaps because occurring earlier in the tradition, are the operatic conventionalisms of Beethoven's youthful *Mit Mädeln sich vertragen* and *Prüfung*, or even the much superior *Adelaide* Op. 46 (recalled at the close of Brahms's *Die Schnur, die Perl an Perle* Op. 57 no. 7); these, in turn, may be related to Schubert's diverse echoes of Rossini.

There were, then, operatic pointers to the *Lied* and a gradual transformation by a new method of setting words and by a fresh kind of response to the text. In this respect it is instructive to compare Schubert's *Suleikas zweiter Gesang* D. 717 with *Suleikas erster Gesang* D. 720. D. 717 is more directly tuneful, its modulations more immediately striking and the coda almost old-fashioned for its time, shaped for good effect at a concert; and, sure enough, it was composed for Anna Milder-Hauptmann, a famous prima donna. But it lacks the intensity of D. 720, which is a truer *Lied* with a climax that, if no less outwardly impressive than the best moments of D. 717, arises from within—not from the need for a rousing, almost theatrical finish.

This kind of subjectivity may be traced back at least to such music as the *Geistliche Lieder* of C. P. E. Bach, to pieces like *Tag und Nacht*, where the compositional resources are not so very different from those of his father's work but the melodic line is more fragmented in response to details in the text. Like the songs of the *Zweite Berliner Liederschule*, however, these were intended for private rather than public use and so were a move towards the nineteenth-century *Lied*; this development was further accentuated by the fact that the *Berliner Liederschule* turned to such poets as Goethe and Klopstock in preference, say, to the dull, moralistic versifying of Gellert. As against these tendencies, their music was often more subservient to the text than that of C. P. E. Bach or even Nichelmann, and as we have seen, Zelter's simplicity was particularly appreciated by poets. This attitude also survived a long time, as is shown by a letter from Beethoven, of all people, to Matthisson, saying 'My dearest wish is gratified if the musical setting is not entirely unworthy of your divine *Adelaide*'.

Josef Haydn was among the first to write out his songs on three staves, thus preparing for a greater elaboration of the keyboard part, while an operatic approach was sometimes retained by Reichardt and Zumsteeg, certain of whose pieces have preludes, postludes, ritornellos for the piano, accompanied recitative, arias at various tempos and even sections of melodrama with the verses spoken over the music (this last being a practice continued in Schumann's Opp. 106 and 122 declamations and in similar Liszt items such as *Des toten Dichters Liebe*). The Zumsteeg and Reichardt pieces led chiefly to secular cantatas like Mendelssohn's *Die erste Walpurgisnacht* Op. 60 and Brahms's *Rinaldo* Op. 50, although a condensation of their method in such works as Mozart's *Das Veilchen* K. 476 also contributed to the *Lied*. The larger, almost sprawling, form was used by Schubert in early pieces like *Der Taucher* D. 111, with its 60-bar piano interlude. He also used it in such later works as *Auf dem Strom* D. 943 and *Der Hirt auf dem Felsen* D. 965; both these works have instrumental obbligatos—for horn and clarinet respectively—that find an echo in the addition of a viola to Brahms's *Gestillte Sehnsucht* and *Geistliches Wiegenlied* Op. 91 nos. 1 and 2.

In many cases, even Schubert's earliest songs take their subjects from German folk myth rather than classical antiquity, and it is noteworthy that even in so late a piece as *Der Hirt auf dem Felsen* D. 965 he is not quite able to reconcile Rossinian *coloratura* with the bucolic accents of Austrian country music: the *Lied*'s turning away from the Berlin composers' more expansive methods was clearly a necessity. The influence of some of Reichardt's simpler pieces, though, can be found in much later songs, even those of Brahms, as will be seen from a comparison between their two settings of Goethe's *Trost in Tränen*, or the way Brahms's *Ruhe, Süssliebchen* Op. 33 no. 9, at its close, echoes the older composer's *Schlaf, Kindchen, schlaf*. There is something of the *Zweite Berliner Liederschule*'s influence, too, in the contrasting tempos of Brahms's expansive *Sind es Schmerzen, sind es Freuden* and *Wie soll ich die Freude, die Wonne denn tragen* Op. 33 nos. 3 and 6.

Mozart's *Das Veilchen* K. 476 is usually cited as a Schubertian song before Schubert, though, as we have seen, the real interest of its pastoral rococo lies in the essential drawing together and condensation of extremely varied elements that went to make up Reichardt's or Zumsteeg's bigger vocal pieces. Even when the condensation is taken so far as in *Als Luise die Briefe ihres ungetreuen Liebhabers verbrannte* K. 520, the experience is still operatically objectified in a character who is distinct from the composer, singer or listener, and this is also true of *An Chloë* K. 524. With each of these songs, and with *Das Lied der Trennung* K. 519 also, one is reminded, despite all the obvious stylistic differences, of the terse little *scenas* of Mussorgsky's Songs and Dances of Death and Without Sunlight cycles. The intimate lyricism of Mozart's *Abendempfindung* K. 523 places it nearer to the nineteenth-century *Lied*, however, with decidedly Schubertian cadences qualifying the still-Italian melodic shapes, and this song is quite untheatrical, as is the less impressive *Das Traumbild* K. 530.

For Beethoven, the song and other small vocal forms were something which, as Wagner wrote, he 'only touched on in passing, as if by experiment.' A few of his songs, like *Vom Tode* and *Die Ehre Gottes aus der Natur* Op. 48 nos. 3 and 4 and, of course, the whole of his *An die ferne Geliebte* cycle Op. 98, anticipate not so much Schubert as a still later Romantic style. This is especially true of *An die ferne Geliebte*, of the Piano Sonata No. 27 Op. 90 and the first movement of the Sonata No. 28 Op. 101, all of which pursue a vein of lyrical meditation

that Beethoven left behind with his next keyboard sonata—
No. 29, the Hammerklavier. Elsewhere he tended to use word-
repetitions more appropriate to aria than to *Lied*; these can be
found in later songs such as the solo versions of Brahms's
Zigeunerlieder Op. 103 nos. 1, 2, 5–8, where whole lines are
repeated, or at the close of the sixth *Magelone Romanze*; more
usual, however, is the case of *Agnes* Op. 59 no. 5, where the
repetitions are not Brahms's and occur in Mörike's original
poem.

Similarly, the ornate vocal parts of several of Loewe's
ballads, such as *Der Blumen Rache* or *Der Nöck*, look back to
florid eighteenth-century opera writing; yet this element
continued to appear, if only occasionally, and however
changed the musical circumstances, in *Lieder* of a much later
date, as at the end of Brahms's *Wie soll ich die Freude, die
Wonne denn tragen* Op. 33 no. 6. The way some of Loewe's keyboard parts elaborated their material, as in *Der Nöck*, or, more
notably, *Edward* (where three definite motives are varied
throughout), was a surer contribution to the *Lied*; this elaboration was developed by Brahms and later Wolf, though it is
notable that the piano is less active in Brahms's ballad-like
duet *Die Nonne und der Ritter* Op. 28 no. 1 than in many of
Loewe's pieces.

The accompaniment's creation of atmosphere in *Ritter Olaf*,
a remarkable dramatic miniature, or in the rapt, intense
Süsses Begräbnis, a true *Lied*, is also relevant here, as is the almost
Sibelian manner in which his *Prinz Eugen* melody only emerges
complete at the close. Loewe had a flair for the supernatural—
Walpurgisnacht, Odins Meeresritt, Der Erlkönig—which is
decidedly Romantic, and his influence on Brahms can be
studied not so much in the Ballads and Romances for two
voices Op. 75 as in a song like *Das Lied vom Herrn von Falkenstein*
Op. 43 no. 4. Note here the leaps of an octave and a fifth, the
way unisons between voice and piano underline the melody's
gesture (as in Schubert's *Die Krähe* from *Die Winterreise* D. 911).
Though descended, through Loewe, from Zelter's and Reichardt's simpler pieces, such unisons always have a specific
purpose with Brahms. In *Trost in Tränen* Op. 48 no. 5, for
example, the keyboard's duplication of the melody prepares
for its continuation of the thread when the voice is silent.

Many other anticipations of Brahms in music from the

quarter century preceding his birth in 1833 could be mentioned. Does not the evocation of a storm in his *So tönet denn, schäumende Wellen* Op. 33 no. 10 hint at the sea scenes of Weber's *Oberon*? Is there not a suggestion of that earlier composer in the final chorus, *Auf dem Meere*, of Brahms's *Rinaldo* Op. 50? Is the *Wiegenlied* Op. 49 no. 4 so familiar that we can scarcely hear its echo of Weber's *Schlaf, Herzenssöhnchen, mein Liebling bist du*, a song with guitar accompaniment written in 1810?

Like the literature of that time, all this music reached towards, and much of it achieved, fresh modes of expression, although often these embodied old principles in new forms. As we have seen, the *Lied* was very far from being a sudden, still less an unexpected discovery. The *durchkomponiertes Lied*, already mentioned in connection with Krufft and other immediate predecessors of nineteenth-century song, dates at least from Caccini and the *Nuove Musiche* of the beginning of the seventeenth century, when it arose, significantly enough, from musicians' desire to achieve a more plastic and more definite expression of their texts. Yet the forest evocations which communicate perhaps the most Germanic of all Romantic moods do appear to have been the discovery of Weber for *Der Freischütz;* these images were taken up by Schumann—*Waldszenen* Op. 82, Wagner—*Waldweben* from *Siegfried*, Liszt—*Waldesrauschen*, and many others. Brahms's *Lieder* reflect this in a most individual way, as *In Waldeseinsamkeit* Op. 85 no. 6 shows, with the twilight nostalgia of *Abenddämmerung* Op. 49 no. 5 as a more oblique example. Also new was the almost legendary flavour encountered in some Romantic works: a section of Schumann's Fantasy Op. 17, perhaps his greatest score, is actually headed '*Im Legendenton*', and this mood is also caught not in Brahms's *Sapphische Ode* Op. 94 no. 4 but in one of his dark-toned viola songs, *Geistliches Wiegenlied* Op. 91 no. 2. New again was the leaning to diabolism already noticed in Loewe but also colouring much larger works such as the operas *Der Vampyr* by Marschner and Meyerbeer's *Robert le Diable*. Even Mendelssohn was affected by this, as his *Die erste Walpurgisnacht* Op. 60 proves; Brahms, aside from an isolated duet also called *Walpurgisnacht* Op. 75 no. 4, and the

23

song *Steig auf, geliebter Schatten* Op. 94 no. 2, did not in this instance respond.

Comparable to these extensions of music's range of expression was the use of regional idioms which, as we have seen, arose partly from growing national consciousness, partly from a renewed interest in the past, and partly also from a desire to break the mould of earlier forms. It has also been remarked that this was less common among German composers, the nature of whose tradition, while able to accommodate many new kinds of resources, acted against any form of exoticism. Brahms's relation to the idioms of German folk song, and his use of supposedly Hungarian styles are discussed later in this book, but it may here be noted that he resorted to other local idioms—though only in his songs and then infrequently. An instance is the rather laboured Spanish mannerisms of *Spanisches Lied* Op. 6 no. 1, and with greater refinement in his mature *Serenade* Op. 58 no. 8. In both cases, however, everything seems to depend on the example of Schumann's *Spanisches Liederspiel* Op. 74 and *Spanische Liebeslieder* Op. 138, not on any music which ever came out of the Iberian peninsula. Slightly more convincing, perhaps because relating to something nearer home, are the Serbian characteristics of *Mädchenlied* Op. 85 no. 3, *Das Mädchen* and *Vorschneller Schwur* Op. 95 nos. 1 and 5, and the Slavonic aspects of *Von ewiger Liebe* Op. 43 no. 1, which has none too distant a cousin in the principal melody of the Adagio to Dvořák's Violin Concerto Op. 53.

Even these minor and comparatively late instances show how attempts were constantly being made to expand the vocabulary of nineteenth-century art music. A previous, and more significant, indication of this new flexibility was that Schubert was able to set over forty poems by Schiller, whom many musicians had considered 'impossible to compose'; before this Beethoven, in his Op. 48 songs, had been more successful with Gellert's verses than had his Berlin predecessors. As in poetry and prose, these changes were gradual and began earlier than at first sight appears. As we have seen, it is a misleading simplification to say that the nineteenth-century *Lied* arose in response to a new literature, for music was a principal source of inspiration to the earlier Romantic authors. At first it may seem surprising that Romantic composers did not continue writing sonatas and comparable pieces with the profusion and regularity of their classical forbears. The sonata idea was the root of so much of Haydn's, Mozart's and Beethoven's finest music yet was apparently of restricted usefulness to men such as Chopin, Schumann or Liszt. The younger Brahms abandoned it—at least so far as his large piano music output was concerned—after his three early sonatas Opp. 1, 2 and 5, and took a very long while to publish his first string quartets (Op. 51) and first symphony (Op. 68). After all, sonata form is architecturally a play of harmonic tensions, a tonal drama, and the Romantics—Brahms again being a good example—showed extreme harmonic sensitivity.

Why did the new composers seek different outlets, if not in new forms then at least in re-evaluations of old ones such as the song? It might be said that for Classical musicians stress between the individual and society's concept of ordered values was symbolically answered by the sonata's resolution of tonal conflict. Yet as we travel from Haydn through Mozart and Beethoven to Schubert tension between the accepted order and the personal will—the composer's desire to express *himself* —grows stronger. The exaltation of subjectivity reached its climax in Wagner's mature operas—not only *Tristan*—and its end in the purely interior drama of such expressionistic masterpieces as Schoenberg's *Erwartung* Op. 17. The beginnings of this process can be heard in pre-Romantic works proper, and prophetically they can be heard most clearly in the piano literature. Clementi's later sonatas include fine music, yet their dramatic elements are too strong for a Mozartian balance of lyric melody and tonal conflict any longer to be possible. In his G minor Sonata Op. 50 no. 3 of 1821 the opening movement's themes do not in themselves really demand the sort of treatment prescribed by his overall tonal plan, and it might be added that this score's romantically subjective motivation is signposted by its subtitle: *Didone abbandonata—scena tragica*. Similarly in Dussek's Sonata in F minor Op. 77, which he named *L'Invocation*, adventurous Romantic harmony (some of it prophetic of Schumann) lessens the impact, and even the meaning, of properly defined tonal conflict. In their keyboard music both Hummel and

Weber interchange quasi-operatic melody with improvisatory virtuosity, their harmonic 'surprise' effects not genuinely arising from structural requirements. The process worked in both directions, for some of Weber's more bravura vocal themes are rather pianistic in shape, while the aimless modulations of Field's sonatas Op. 1, admittedly composed when he was only nineteen, mark a further stage of structural fragmentation.

By, say, 1820 the sonata had been replaced in progressive musical circles by small works. Schubert's Impromptus D. 899, 935 and 946 and *Moments musicaux* D. 780 are the commonly cited instances of the process, but there are many others, some of them unjustly neglected, such as Tomášek's *Eclogues* Opp. 35, 39, 47, 51, 53, 66 and 83 and *Dithyrambs* Opp. 52 and 65 (note the Greek-derived titles), that were equally characteristic of the Romantically subjective current. An idea of the process of condensation may be got by comparing, say, Beethoven's *Der Wachtelschlag* Op. 32 no. 2 of 1804, which elaborates its material over six pages with various tempo changes, with Schubert's simple 1822 strophic setting of the same text (D. 742). Also typifying the exploration of personal feeling are Field's *Nocturnes*, their elegiac lyricism, though derived from Italian opera, pointing to the melancholy self-communing of Brahms's late Intermezzos Opp. 116–19. It is relevant, also, that some of the slow movements of Brahms's larger works, like those by Schubert before him and Mahler later, are modelled on the song, not the aria, hymn or chorale.

If the piano—which never deserved Voltaire's dismissal as 'A kettle-maker's invention'—emerged as this period's dominant instrument this is partly because its nearly orchestral range of sonorities made it so apt for the Romantics' desire for harmonic discovery. At the same time, the new virtuosity also became a form of emotional exploration, as Liszt, Schumann and later Brahms with his Variations Op. 35 acknowledged with piano works based on Paganini's fantastic *Capriccios*. Before that, Schubert had proved how vividly the keyboard might reflect and indeed enhance the drama and poetry of songs, and its evocative power led to the dualism of the new *Lieder*, which perhaps more than any other single factor distinguished them from any predecessors. This equal partnership between voice and piano is quite different in its effect from anything found in, say, Dowland's lute songs, which though passionate as any *Lied* are not dramatic, their emotion being communicated almost entirely by the vocal line. Another aspect of the *Lied*'s duality is that it makes narrative and emotional expression simultaneous, whereas in the more elaborate songs of Reichardt and Zumsteeg, or in opera and oratorio, they usually alternate. Schubert's *Die junge Nonne* D. 828 is a fine instance of the *Lied*'s balance of lyricism and symbolic personal drama; the composer's involvement with his character is far more direct, more immediate than, say, Mozart's objective though humane attitude to his operatic personages—to Fiordiligi or Figaro, to Dorabella or Don Giovanni.

Romanticism's emphasis on subjective and emotional factors was indeed highly sympathetic to the *Lied*, for in this music, even though it is very much a part of the German tradition, the listener's response is stimulated directly rather than through the dialectical subtleties of musical argument. However, such a generalization at once leads one to think of exceptions, such as the three-part counterpoint of Schubert's *Vom Mitleiden Maria* D. 632, the ingenious thematic development of Brahms's *Mein wundes Herz verlangt nach milder Ruh* Op. 59 no. 7 (which again employs counterpoint, including diminution), or the canons of his duet *Phänomen* Op. 61 no. 3. More will be said later on such questions as thematic development, the use of counterpoint, and so on, when consideration is given to the elements of Brahms's compositional craft in his songs.

Equality of partnership between voice and piano meant that the *Lied*'s word-painting—the music's response to individual words and phrases rather than to a text's general atmosphere—is often extremely vivid, but this also has a long ancestry. Instances from the English and Italian madrigals and from Bach's cantatas need hardly be cited, although it may be noted that the practice goes back at least to Jacob Obrecht and Josquin des Prés in the fifteenth century. More relevant to Brahms and his contemporaries were such things as the descriptive passages in Haydn's *The Creation* or the opera orchestration of Mozart, where in *Così fan tutte* the woodwind pervades that whole score, suggesting the sea and sun, with clarinets, often in warm, sensuous thirds, associated with

Fiordiligi and Dorabella, the detached, nasal-sounding oboes with Don Alfonso. This was taken further by Weber, especially in *Der Freischütz*, with its low flutes for Samiel and clarinets for Agathe.

The *Lieder* composers needed musically to underline the meanings of their texts in a way that was immediately effective because of the small scale on which they were working; this led to further harmonic experiment paralleling the exploration of personal feeling so evident in Romantic solo piano music. Perhaps this is more immediately apparent in the songs and keyboard pieces of Schumann and Liszt than in Brahms. Yet the latter's quotation of *'Batti, batti'* from Mozart's *Don Giovanni* (a melody which also makes a brief appearance during Beethoven's Quintet Op. 16) in *Liebe und Frühling* Op. 3 no. 2 is a kind of symbolical indication of his links with the older music, just as the D minor of his Tragic Overture Op. 81 suggests that his feeling for key related to Mozart's (e.g. in the Piano Concerto No. 20 K. 466). A quotation of similar import to that in *Liebe und Frühling*, one feels, is Brahms's reference, already mentioned, to the chorale melody *O Haupt voll Blut und Wunden* in *Auf dem Kirchhofe* Op. 105 no. 4. Comments by Hoffmann on Mozart's music (in *Der Dichter und der Komponist* of 1813) such as 'The mysterious language of a distant spiritual kingdom, whose marvellous accents echo in our innermost being, arousing a higher, more intense life', his eulogizing of Beethoven, and Spohr's naming of Mozart, in his *Autobiography*, as his main operatic guide show that to such literary and musical Romantics the earlier masters were Romantic too. Mozart's *Die Zauberflöte*, in particular, influenced not only Goethe, who wrote a sequel—*Die zauberflöte, Zweiter Teil*—but also Tieck's *Gestiefelter Kater*, Schlegel's *Ehrenpforte* and Grillparzer's *Der Traum ein Leben*. In their many backward- and forward-looking aspects Brahms's *Lieder* are indeed a single thread in a continuous network whose proportions can merely be suggested here; one is reminded of Büchner, the brief scenes of whose *Woyzeck* besides looking back to the *Sturm und Drang* also anticipate the Expressionist drama of our own century.

A study of Schumann's critical writings—and he was a recognized leader among German musical Romantics—will show that despite its greatly increased use of smaller forms as vehicles for the most significant musical thought, and whatever might have been the prevailing ideas in equivalent literary circles, the movement was certainly not conceived as a conscious revolt against classical virtues. The Romantics' belief that they were continuing a tradition was emphasized by use of the term 'neo-Romantic' from 1833 (the year of Brahms's birth) onwards, although this did not become general usage until 1839, when Becker's musical novel *Der Neuromantiker* appeared. Schumann's study of Bach and his views on him might seem one-sided in the light of modern scholarship (as, no doubt, would those of Chopin or Brahms) yet they affect the textures of some of his most lyrical keyboard pieces. He had, however, considerable reservations about the term 'Romantic' and his 1835 reviews of, say, Ferdinand Hiller's Studies Op. 15 or of Berlioz's *Symphonie fantastique* analyse these scores in extreme detail. This proves his concern with formal clarity, exactness of harmonic diction and the other traditional German musical virtues—which are sometimes less conspicuous in his own works, particularly his songs, certain of which seem improvisatory compared with those of Schubert or Brahms.

However, despite this insistence on traditional values even in the face of the re-orientations of Romanticism, and despite the exclusive nature of German musical culture, a few incidental outside influences may be detected. German composers were impressed, for example, by the post-Gluck operas of Cherubini and Méhul, as they were later by Spontini; Beethoven particularly admired Cherubini, and in general terms his *Fidelio* reflects the example of *Léonore* by Gaveaux and of Paër's *Leonora*. In Brahms, too, besides the operatic echoes already mentioned in some of his *Lieder*, one may note the rather marginal Italianism of his choral Ave Maria Op. 12 or that reference to Viotti's A minor Violin Concerto in the first movement of his Double Concerto Op. 102, the reminiscences of Pergolesi's *Ninetta* in *Die Spröde* Op. 58 no. 3, further such long-range Italianisms as the way the Scherzo of his Piano Sonata No. 3 Op. 5 reminds us of Mendelssohn's C minor Trio Op. 66 (1845) which in turn echoes Legrenzi's *Che fiero costume*. Such things have a small place in Brahms's music, however, and though again one might point to the Italianate thirds of

Serenade Op. 58 no. 8, the sixths of *Sind es Schmerzen, sind es Freuden* Op. 33 no. 3 or of *Frühlingstrost* Op. 63 no. 1 really are more characteristic, and have no specifically southern overtones. Later we find, as might be expected, more extreme cases such as the songs of Wolf's *Italienisches Liederbuch*, which are wholly Austro-German and carry hints of no other tradition. Yet Brahms was to a remarkable extent, even more than Wagner, the most purely Teutonic artist since Dürer, and both his music and his personality reflect this with a directness which at times is almost disconcerting. Surely no other musician can have been photographed in a textbook to a illustrate classic racial type, yet Kalbeck, his friend and biographer, tells us that Brahms's portrait was so used, to exemplify the Teuton in a primer by Velhagen and Klasing. (The composer himself spoke of this to Widmann, who says it was a geography book.)

Brahms's life—he was born in 1833 and died in 1897—almost entirely covered a period during which Germany changed profoundly, these changes centring, as in several other areas of Europe, around the failure of the revolutionary movement of 1848. Indeed, it is hard to see much outward similarity between the Germany of 1820, the land of Novalis, Tieck and Hoffmann, and that of 1870 and the onslaught on France, a country it would seem more apt to associate with such figures as Bismarck and von Moltke. Unlikely as it may appear, Brahms reflected these changes himself; it is difficult to find many outward links between the youth of twenty who, in a contemporary account, was 'Shy, retiring, modest, of delicate mien, with blue eyes, fair hair, the voice of a girl, still unbroken, and a face like a child's' (an almost exact description, this, of a hero from Novalis or Richter) and the man of fifty who, in later contemporary accounts, would eat a whole tin of sardines with his fingers and pour the oil down his throat, or who would leave a room saying 'If there's anyone here I haven't insulted then I beg his pardon.'

Comparable shifts of emphasis have been noted in the music of other German composers such as Richard Strauss, whose drastic expansion of orchestral resources, following the restraint of his youthful works, has been related to the change that came with the accession of Wilhelm II in 1888, when a more heavily armed Germany embarked on imperialist adventures. Perhaps it is not unduly far-fetched to draw a parallel between Germany's highly efficient industrialization and the complex, detailed precision of Strauss's orchestra; but no other music embodies duality and sudden change through and through as does that of Brahms, even though it belies, as art usually does, the relative simplicities of physical and political change.

Many of the sharp contrasts found in his pieces are unremarkable and arise from the text: the differentiation between the two couples' moods in *Wechsellied zum Tanze* Op. 31 no. 1, the daughter's sadness and the firmness of the mother in *Der Kranz* Op. 84 no. 2, question and answer in *Jägerlied* Op. 66 no. 4, the first three and the last two verses of *Todessehnen* Op. 86 no. 6, the sudden quaver motion at the mention of the singer's oath in *Unüberwindlich* Op. 72 no. 5, or, simpler still, the effect of full harmony after unison in *Nun steh'n die Rosen in Blüthe* Op. 44 no. 7. Many composers had resorted to greater extremes than these—for instance, the brook music which follows the storm in Schubert's *Im Walde* D. 708, or the shift from stillness to expectancy in *Jägers Abendlied* D. 368. With Brahms contrast evolves chiefly on the harmonic and rhythmic planes whereas, say, in Beethoven it works more through melody, dynamics and orchestration. This is not to suggest that there was anything new in the idea of contrast, yet its exploitation in such music does embody a highly Romantic principle, first preached in this connection, perhaps, in the Preface to Victor Hugo's *Cromwell* six years prior to Brahms's birth. Berlioz, too, could write much later, in 1865, that 'Music lives only by contrast', while a similar idea clearly informs the painting of Delacroix.

With Brahms, however, it was a more personal matter—more directly a result of his own circumstances than of any theory. Joachim said, in an 1856 letter, 'Brahms has two personalities: one predominantly of childlike genius . . . and the other of demoniac cunning which, with an icy surface, suddenly breaks forth in a pedantic, prosaic compulsion to dominate.' Similarly, Billroth, who was a close friend of Brahms from 1865 to 1894, could write to his daughter Else, after the composer had behaved particularly badly at an important dinner party in 1892: 'It makes no difference to him whether serious men are present who value him greatly or whether he has a gang of rascals for audience . . . I cannot find a bridge between his deep seriousness and this sort of behaviour in serious company. He enjoys teasing and baiting people sometimes; it appears to be a necessity for him. Perhaps it is a remnant of the resentment which has survived from his youth, when, knowing how serious his compositions were, he was not accepted, and had works scorned which he had written with his life's blood. . . . According to his biographers, Beethoven must have been rather the same. It was in his character that when happy he was like a child and had no greater pleasure than to fool people. This also applies to Wagner, who in his humorous moods was childlike, awkward and uncouth. At any rate, this evening has robbed me of any wish to undertake anything similar with Brahms again. He really does make it very hard for one to keep on loving him.'

This duality is especially apparent in Brahms's letters, with their evidence of his loyalty to friends, tender love of children, quiet (virtually secret) benefactions to those in need, his humour, and his longing for a settled existence—all flatly contradicting the porcupine exterior. An unwillingness to take risks in music or in life is also plain, and he was reluctant to enter into any situation whose outcome he could not clearly see from the beginning. Brahms achieved success but at the cost of loneliness: he remained a bachelor living in furnished rooms, and it was inevitable as the years passed that unresolved inner conflicts should express themselves as bad temper and rudeness. Brahms was of North German working-class Protestant stock and his natural stolidity and tenaciousness were intensified, as Billroth guessed, by a hard childhood. Among exalted circles in Vienna, or even as a young man at Detmold, he was sometimes as arrogant and offensive as Beethoven, yet for the opposite reason. As certain of *his* letters make clear, Beethoven exalted in the pride of his spirit, whereas Brahms was apprehensive of the fire within himself.

The nineteenth-century partisans of Bruckner versus Brahms were wrong about the irreconcilable differences between their music—both were late Romantics working well inside the same German tradition—yet beneath obvious similarities they represent opposite poles of temperament: Bruckner was single-minded and simple-hearted, Brahms in essence a contradiction. Hence the often violent misunderstandings with old friends, even with Clara Schumann and Joachim, the obscurities of Brahms's letters and conversation, and his need for friends who although as successful as himself were more extroverted—such as Billroth, who was an internationally famous surgeon. Perhaps this was also the reason why he admired the novels of Gottfried Keller, who, especially in the partly autobiographical *Bildungsroman* called *Der grüne Heinrich*, is concerned with people who although of mature years have, through suppressing the voice of nature, failed to develop their true potentialities.

Brahms once spoke of the Alto Rhapsody Op. 53 as a 'sequel' to the carefree *Liebeslieder* Waltzes Op. 52; insofar as the former, a setting of Goethe, portrays a lone wanderer lost in the wilderness and with incurable pain in his heart, this implies a forbidding view of life. Plenty of gloomy verses have been set by other composers, some of them quite morbid, such as Schubert's *Vor meiner Wiege* D. 927, but certain of Brahms's later choices, including the texts of *Beim Abschied* Op. 95 no. 3, *Ein Wanderer* Op. 106 no. 5 and *Mädchenlied* Op. 107 no. 5, all expressing isolation amid the company of others, seem particularly significant. Brahms's duality is apparent in many pairs of opuses, not least between the *Liebeslieder* and the preceding String Quartets Op. 51, especially the grim outer movements of No. 1 in C minor; other cases are his D minor Piano Concerto Op. 15, which was immediately followed by the genial, if somewhat negative, Serenade Op. 16, the E minor Cello Sonata Op. 38 (every theme of which first appears in a minor key) tailed by the Op. 39 Waltzes for piano, and the *Zigeunerlieder* Op. 103 that follow close on the heels of the Double Concerto Op. 102.

This also applies to the sets of *Lieder* for solo voice. The nine songs of Op. 32 dealing with getting old having achieved nothing, and with devotion to an unresponsive beloved and again achieving nothing, are followed by the untrammelled exuberance of the Op. 33 set with their romantic tale of '*Der schönen Magelone und des Grafen Peter*'. A further example is provided by the fact that immediately afterwards Brahms followed the chamber music austerities of his Piano Quintet Op. 34 with the Paganini Variations Op. 35, most extrovert of his keyboard works. Again, with his final group of songs, the

33

Vier ernste Gesänge Op. 121, Brahms passes the boundaries of normal *Lieder* writing yet in his next and indeed last work, the posthumously published Op. 122, immediately reverts to the conservative form of the chorale prelude for organ. Similarly, his Opp. 94 and 95 sets would hardly seem expressive of the same outlook on life; the warmth of *Sapphische Ode* (No. 4) apart, Op. 94 is very sombre while Op. 95 is light and full of charm.

Often it is the same with adjacent songs within a particular opus. Notice the contrasts between the two *Liebe und Frühling* settings of Op. 3 or between the two *Weg der Liebe* duets of Op. 20, the immediate repose of *Wie schnell verschwindet so Licht als Glanz* Op. 33 no. 11 after the raging storm of No. 10, *So tönet denn, schäumende Wellen.* With the Reinhold verses chosen for Op. 97 nos. 1 and 2, in No. 1 the 'Nachtigall' of the title indirectly evokes reluctant nostalgia for the past while in No. 2, *Auf dem Schiffe*, an unspecified 'Vögelein' represents simpler aspirations. More direct is the case of Brahms's *Abendständchen* and *Vineta* Op. 42 nos. 1 and 2—essays in the style of Schumann's romantic part songs—whose atmospheric effect is contradicted by *Darthulas Grabesgesang* Op. 42 no. 3, which opens and closes like a sixteenth-century antiphonal chorus. Also worth noting is the contrast between the expansiveness of *Vom Strande* Op. 69 no. 6 and the concise simplicity of *Über die See* Op. 69 no. 7.

Taken together, all these cases suggest greater interior conflict than do the oppositions of Schumann's Florestan and Eusebius,* and this becomes more evident as soon as we look at individual works. Consider, for example, the light-hearted first movement of the String Quintet No. 2 Op. 111, immediately contradicted by a tragic *Adagio* (which, via the equivalent movement of Mendelssohn's String Quintet Op. 87, relates to the *Adagio* of Beethoven's String Quartet No. 7 Op. 59 no. 1), or the way the finale's jaunty cello tune in the Piano Quintet Op. 34 is preceded by a darkly brooding introduction of forty-one bars. It is the same in Brahms's *Lieder*, as is shown by the contrasting middle section of *Ruhe, Süssliebchen* Op. 33 no. 9, or in *Unbewegte laue Luft* Op. 57 no. 8 where nature's dreamy

---

* Florestan and Eusebius were the two personae Schumann thought of as polarizing the contradictory opposites of his own nature. Florestan was fiery and active, Eusebius the remote dreamer.

peacefulness, conveyed by trills and pastoral phrases, is set against man's passion in the second half; a further example is *Waldeseinsamkeit* Op. 85 no. 6, where the emotional modulations of the middle part contrast with serene harmonies at the close.

To these may be added Brahms's contrast between the sentimental and the passionately declamatory in *Sehnsucht* Op. 49 no. 3 and, on a different level, the interchange of 3/4 with 9/8 during *Freiwillige her!* Op. 41 no. 2. More abrupt is the shift from 4/4 to 15/4 (as 9/4 + 6/4) in *Marias Wallfahrt* Op. 22 no. 3, or, on a larger scale, from the *tranquillo* passage to the final climax of the first movement of his *Triumphlied* Op. 55. Also noteworthy is *Therese* Op. 86 no. 1, an unusual juxtaposition of simplicity and mystery, in which the first two verses are in quasi-folk song style but the third and last, taking advantage of the wayward ending of the second, is freer altogether, in a new key and with a syncopated accompaniment. More concentrated examples of this are the touch of bitterness injected at the close of *Die Spröde* Op. 58 no. 3 and the hollowness at the end of *Immer leiser wird mein Schlummer* Op. 105 no. 2. Less convincing—and disruptive of unity—are the mood changes of *Schwermut* and *Vorüber* Op. 58 nos. 5 and 7. Perhaps a more revealing contrast than any of these, however, is in *Rinaldo* Op. 50, where a decidedly Wagnerian setting of the words 'In glänzender Pracht' is promptly followed by a dutiful, very Brahmsian *fugato*!

These extremes are in turn qualified by the composer's innate caution, and so, despite its many sharp contrasts, his music often takes us by stealth rather than through immediate impact. Indeed, despite all this he conscientiously tried to avoid extremes, or at least to reconcile them, and, as a generalization, his tempo directions became more cautious as the years passed. The *allegro con brio* was hardly the most natural mode of expression for one of Brahms's fundamentally lyric, contemplative temperament, still less the *prestissimo*, and there is nothing in his *Lieder* comparable to the seventeen tempo changes in eighteen pages of Schubert's *Eine Leichenphantasie* D. 7. It is another contradiction that despite the remarkable exuberance of his early works, especially the vast piano sonatas Opp. 1, 2 and 5, his caution appeared early, for he even burned the exercises he wrote while studying with Marxsen, and regularly destroyed mature compositions that failed to satisfy him; not many great composers have left behind so few unpublished manuscripts or sketches as Brahms. Related to this is his opposition to the idea of the *Gesamtausgabe* —the complete edition of a composer's output including even the earliest pieces—which he made clear in letters to Elisabet von Herzogenberg and to La Mara written during 1885. Brahms's caution is further exemplified by his deference to the advice of others; he submitted mature scores such as the Requiem Op. 45 for Marxsen's approval and, much later, he sought Joachim's help while writing the Double Concerto Op. 102 of 1887.

The benefits of Brahms's fusion of opposites can be heard in many places, such as the first section of his *Nänie* Op. 82, with its combination of pastoral and polyphonic elements. In other choral works, too, there is an unpedantic reconciliation of old and new resources, of rhythmic and harmonic innovations together with reminders of the Baroque. Indeed, following such precedents as the finale to Mozart's 'Linz' Symphony K. 425, he united classical craftsmanship and certain Baroque attitudes towards counterpoint. Further, he utilized all the potentialities of a thematic idea together with the Romantic concept of musical expressiveness by the use of harmonic, colouristic and textural resources. Thus he fused some of the finest elements of eighteenth and nineteenth-century music— and this without stylistic incongruity or the use of antiquated techniques divorced from the living musical language of his time. Though not on the same level, this is comparable with Beethoven's late synthesis of sonata, fugue and variation, and, as a characteristic nineteenth-century achievement, has parallels in the work of composers supposedly following quite different paths from Brahms. Instances of such integration are Saint-Saëns' Symphony No. 3 Op. 78 and the finale of Bruckner's No. 5, which begins with memories of themes from earlier movements, combines the material in a double fugue which has elements of sonata form and ends with a chorale. Other cases such as Liszt's *Grosses Konzertsolo* or his Sonata also relate to Brahms's tendency to combine more than one movement; this is typified in his String Quintet No. 1 Op. 88 and Violin Sonata No. 2 Op. 100, which, like Berwald's earlier

Symphony No. 3 *Singulière*, unite Scherzo and slow movement; the variations of the Clarinet Sonata Op. 120 no. 2, which serve both as slow movement and finale is a further example. This had been anticipated in a few works such as Schubert's Fantasy in F minor D. 940 for piano duet, and was later taken further by Schoenberg, among others, in his String Quartet No. 1 Op. 7 and Piano Concerto Op. 42. The process of combination affected other quite different facets of music such as nationalistic traits, and resulted in the Franco-Russian style of Stravinsky's early ballets, in the Germanic works of a Frenchman such as Florent Schmitt, and so on.

In its contrapuntal aspect Brahms's synthesis depended less on J. S. Bach than on Handel; the influence of his Dettingen Te Deum is very apparent in the *Triumphlied* Op. 55, and in this, like other nineteenth-century composers, he followed Beethoven, who was particularly influenced by Handel in his overture 'The Consecration of the House' Op. 124 and the fugal sections of the *Missa Solemnis* Op. 123. This tendency became quite widespread, as is suggested by the Handelian influence on Schubert's *Der Winterabend* D. 938 and a number of works such as Moscheles's *Hommage à Handel* Op. 92 for two pianos. But generally speaking nineteenth-century German composers, following a tendency already apparent in some earlier works, such as the fugues of W. F. Bach, substituted a harmonically-inspired polyphony for true counterpoint; and even in a piece like the fugue which so triumphantly crowns Brahms's Op. 24 Variations on a Theme of Handel (not J. S. Bach) we miss the tension between the lines and their implied harmony which generates so much of the impact of Bach's music. Similarly the counterpoint of Mendelssohn's Preludes and Fugues Op. 35 is quite un-Bachian, and though Wagner best typifies nineteenth-century polyphony and departs farthest from the set procedures of the older counterpoint, there are pages in *Parsifal* especially which have more in common with the spirit of Johann Sebastian's technique than almost anything in Brahms. However, there are exceptions, such as Brahms's A flat minor organ Fugue (no opus number) and some of the Op. 122 Chorale Preludes, also for organ. Here the instrument may well have influenced the contrapuntal style, but in such movements as the fugal finale to the String Quintet No. 1 Op. 88 Brahms demonstrably took as his model the fugues of the last piano sonatas and string quartets of Beethoven. Beethoven similarly is the model for the fugal finale to the Op. 38 Cello Sonata, despite its relationship with Contrapunctus XIII of Bach's *Art of the Fugue*. Brahms's polyphonic tendencies were taken further by Reger, and it is notable that even in this composer's most highly detailed textures the flow of the parts is usually subordinate to the harmonic richness of the whole, rather as the individuality of Brahms's motets depends more on their harmony than on their contrapuntal technique, remarkable though this latter is.

A drive towards synthesis, towards a fusion of the opposites almost involuntarily produced by his music, can be detected repeatedly in Brahms. Following the marked differences between the two sets of *Lieder* Opp. 32 and 33 noted above, his next group of songs, Op. 43, attempts an integration of the two, drawing on the qualities of both. Similarly, after the contrast between his Opp. 94 and 95 sets, Opp. 96 and 97, while again having certain differences, are considerably more uniform in mood and approach. Of much greater significance, however, than any specific technical or stylistic features is the conflict between Romantic individuality and Teutonic stolidity which informs nearly all the oppositions of Brahms's work. Often this is expressed as a struggle between lyrical and dramatic entities, as in the opening movement of his Violin Concerto Op. 77, where an undercurrent of aggression prevents the music from luxuriating into too painful a nostalgia while at the same time lyricism curbs undue exuberance.

Such resolutions at once remind us of Schubert in whose music there is often a more explicit conflict between lyrical dream and aggressive reality, between a yearning for the Viennese past and struggle with the world as it is. Sometimes the opposition is between his lyrical, Romantic temperament and the dramatic, classical nature of his material—an aspect of the breakdown of larger forms in the earlier part of the nineteenth century discussed above. Schubert's song melodies are self-contained (rather than material for Beethovenian development) and his romantic harmony, with its emotionally exploratory modulations, produced rhapsodic effects apt for the small canvas of a *Lied* but disruptive of symphonic processes.

He matured earlier as a song writer than as a symphonist, and significantly the case was still more extreme with Brahms, who composed his first outstanding song, *Liebestreu* Op. 3 no. 1, at eighteen but his first symphony, Op. 68, only at forty-three. It is not surprising that an early Schubert symphony like No. 4 in C minor D. 417 should owe more to Beethoven's String Quartet Op. 18 no. 4 than to his C minor Symphony or sonatas, but in the finale there are the highly Schubertian alternations between major and minor through which he so often conveyed his strange equivocations between innocence and experience. This device assumed especial importance in his later music, as the Fantasy in F minor D. 940 for piano duet shows, and became structural in, for example, the G major String Quartet D. 887. It had a precedent in such things as the C major/minor of Mozart's *Missa Solemnis* K. 337 and was duly echoed in a number of Brahms's orchestral movements such as the Allegretto grazioso of his Symphony No. 2 Op. 73, besides frequently occurring with other composers like Bruckner and later still Mahler (first movement of Symphony No. 9—1909).

Yet Schubert's practice in his songs is perhaps most relevant to Brahms. Consider how in *Die Rose* D. 745 the hovering between major and minor reflects the flower's welcoming and shrinking from the sun's light, and how the music turns permanently to the minor when the flower's brief life is over; or how in *Rückblick* from *Die Winterreise* D. 911 it echoes in turn the lover's haste to leave the fateful town and its past happy associations. So with Brahms, the doubt in the singer's words at the end of *Spanisches Lied* Op. 6 no. 1 is expressed by an interchange of major and minor, as is separation from the beloved at the close of *Muss es eine Trennung geben* Op. 33 no. 12, or the unease of *Nachtwandler* Op. 86 no. 3; other cases are *Die Trauernde* Op. 7 no. 5, and *O liebliche Wangen* Op. 47 no. 4 where the hovering between major and minor at the conclusion of each verse has particular effect.

Brahms's ability to extend songlike melodic ideas into thematic lines also relates to Schubert, and at the same time his direct use of material from his *Lieder* in his instrumental works is part of his attempt to dissolve song in tonal drama, to reconcile the opposites yet again. Examples are the appearances of *Komm bald* Op. 97 no. 5 and *Wie Melodien zieht es*

Op. 105 no. 1 in the Violin Sonata No. 2 Op. 100, of *Todes-sehnen* Op. 86 no. 6 in the Piano Concerto No. 2 Op. 83 and the close resemblance between the cello's theme in the Andante of this concerto and the melody of *Immer leiser wird mein Schlummer* Op. 105 no. 2. Another case is the link between his *Academic Festival Overture* Op. 80 and the songs *Frühlingslied* Op. 85 no. 5 and *Ständchen* Op. 106 no. 1. The echo of Beethoven's Piano Sonata No. 14 Op. 27 no. 2 'Moonlight' in *Nachklang* Op. 59 no. 4 shows Brahms obliquely using one of his major influences to the same end, as do the reminiscences of the Adagio to Beethoven's Piano Sonata No. 17 Op. 31 no. 2 'Tempest' in the accompaniment of the seventh Magelone song, *War es dir, dem diese Lippen bebten* Op. 33.

Yet despite these and other salutations he remained a naturally lyrical composer, and a symphonic/sonata one only by relentless self-discipline. Regarding his difficulties with the orchestra it is worth recalling Richard Strauss's comment in his revision of Berlioz's *Traité d'Instrumentation* that although 'the spirit of the piano' informs Beethoven's symphonies, it 'completely dominates' the orchestral music of Schumann and Brahms. This is a sweeping generalization yet of obvious interest when coming from an acknowledged master of the orchestra, and Brahms's correspondence with Joachim shows that even as late as 1887, with all his orchestral works achieved, he still felt most at home writing for the piano rather than for more ambitious combinations. The fact that his Symphony No. 1 Op. 68, premièred in 1876, is mentioned in an 1863 letter to Dietrich gives an idea of what a protracted and arduous task its composition was.

Characteristic of Brahms's larger structures is that the finale of this work conveys more of a desire to be joyful than a true surrender to joy, while the famous 'big tune' is almost theatrical, rather than symphonic. The coda's exultation is also unconvincing, and Clara Schumann perceptively wrote to the composer, 'I do feel that musically the *Presto* . . . falls a bit flat. To me its intensification appears to be in external rather than internal emotion: it somehow does not organically evolve from the whole.' Similarly, the finale of his Symphony No. 2 Op. 73 offers not jubilation but a quasi-classical stylization of it. And just as the overall shape of the finale to No. 1 rather too closely resembles that of the last movement of

Beethoven's No. 9, so the opening Allegro of the Piano Concerto No. 2 Op. 83 too noticeably parallels that of Beethoven's Emperor Concerto; the fugue of the Handel Variations Op. 24, triumphant conclusion though it is, seems too directly reminiscent of the finale to Beethoven's Hammerklavier Sonata Op. 106.

Schumann called Brahms's youthful piano sonatas 'symphonies in disguise' (*verschleierte Symphonien*), yet the opening Beethovenian gesture of the Sonata No. 2 Op. 2 does not really lead anywhere structurally despite its show of energy, and the point is confirmed by the first movement of the Op. 1 Sonata, where the fullest treatment is given not to the very rhythmic first subject (reminiscent this time of the openings of the Hammerklavier Sonata Op. 106 and of Schubert's 'Wanderer' Fantasy D. 760) but to the lyrical second. Again, in the finale to Brahms's Piano Sonata No. 3 Op. 5 it is the chorale-type melody of the second episode which has the last word, and elsewhere in these works, despite all their outward-going power, the composer is most himself in the lyrical passages, such as the Andante of Op. 5, or the main theme of the finale to Op. 2.

It is also significant that ten of Brahms's thirteen orchestral works date from just one phase of his development—the years 1873–87—whereas the more congenial forms of song, piano and chamber music occur throughout his entire professional life and so give a far more complete idea of the real nature of his gifts. Even the big accompanied choral works preceded the bulk of Brahms's symphonic production, a sign of his preference for vocal rather than orchestral writing, but it is noteworthy that after the *Triumphlied* Op. 55 which dates from 1870–71, there were no choral pieces in more than one movement; this again suggests his liking for smaller, lyrical forms.

In the large orchestral works, and sometimes in his chamber music also, there is rather too great a family likeness among Brahms's second subjects, excellent though these usually are in themselves. Also there are rather too many arpeggio themes, to which individuality is not always imparted by the underlying harmony. Here Brahms failed to learn from Beethoven, whose second—let alone first—subjects often have so pronounced a character that they are still recognizable if reduced to their rhythm alone. In few cases would this be true of Brahms's inventions, and this because of their lyrical emphasis and despite the fact that his contrasts work on a rhythmic level to a greater extent than Beethoven's. This is less paradoxical than it appears when we remember that Brahms's rhythmic vocabulary, like Schubert's, largely arose in a lyrical context—through the setting of words. Yet even here there is a distinction, for whereas Schubert will often put his themes in a fresh harmonic setting without altering their rhythmic pattern, the reverse is frequently true of Brahms. The latter's rhythmic variations are in this respect worthy of comparison with those of Wagner, but their purpose remains lyrical rather than dramatic, and so an insufficient answer to the symphonic problem.

Brahms's fusion of formally Baroque and classical with lyrically Romantic elements was not always successful, even outside the symphonic context, as is shown by the rather self-conscious contrapuntal ingenuities of his Variations on a Theme of Schumann Op. 9, especially the tenth variation, or by another piano work, his Intermezzo Op. 118 no. 4 where the canon though ingeniously carried through is not really spontaneous. A further such case is the opening Andante moderato section of his *a cappella* motet *Schaffe in mir, Gott* Op. 29 no. 2, where the bass, moving at half the speed, is an exact augmentation of the soprano line. At such moments one can sympathize with Weingartner, who had 'Repeatedly and diligently studied the greatest part of his work', describing Brahms's music as 'scientific' in his 1897 lecture *The Symphony after Beethoven*, for though formal processes can help a composer shape his thought they can also distort the originality of his idea.

It is typical of the way Brahms sought to bring extremes together that some of the happiest uses of contrapuntal resource occur in the purely lyrical context of his *Lieder*. Examples are the canonic development between the voices in the duet *Am Strande* Op. 66 no. 3, the counterpoint between voice and piano bass, expressive of the singer's devotion and the beloved's indifference, in *An die Stolze* Op. 107 no. 1, or even the moments of canonic ingenuity in the accompaniment of *All mein Gedanken*, No. 30 of the *49* (so-called) *Deutsche Volkslieder*. Although the very careful organization of specific

42

Brahms songs will be discussed later, it may be said here that even the largest of the *Magelone Romanzen* Op. 33, his most expansive songs, are not symphonic in their structure, and even in a complex setting such as *Liebe kam aus fernen Landen* Op. 33 no. 4 lyricism predominates. The indulgent long notes at the repeated 'ein Lichtstrahl in der Dämmerung' in No. 1, *Keinen hat es noch gereut*, are noteworthy because it is characteristic of Brahms to make so nostalgic an emphasis before all the adventures described in the rest of the cycle have begun. Even in the *Vier ernste Gesänge* Op. 121 his softer side finally prevails.

Revealing also is a comparison between *Du sprichst, dass ich mich täuschte* Op. 32 no. 6 with Schubert's setting of a slightly different version of Platen's verses, *Du liebst mich nicht* D. 756, for, lyrical composer though he was, Schubert's version is more dramatic; similarly in *Sapphische Ode* Op. 94 no. 4 Brahms adapts the ending of Schubert's *Am Meer* D. 957, but puts it to less dramatic use. It is chiefly the overriding lyricism which makes his *Edward* Op. 75 no. 1 inferior to Loewe's dramatically evocative setting; to take an example from another area of Brahms's work altogether, even in the outer movements of his String Quartet No. 1 Op. 51 no. 1, which are among the most deliberately austere of all his pages, lyricism can still be felt glowing beneath the music's surface, generating power through its very suppression.

These C minor String Quartet movements are a result, as are the equivalent parts of his Symphony No. 1 Op. 68 in the same key, of too grim a determination to emulate the driving logic of Beethoven's music. Brahms's veneration for Beethoven derived from Marxsen (whose orchestration of the Kreutzer Sonata Op. 47, performed in Hamburg during 1835, might well have been an interesting document), but the dissimilarities of their temperaments are never in doubt. An outward parallel has already been noted, for instance, between the opening phrases of Brahms's Op. 1 and Beethoven's Hammerklavier Op. 106 sonatas, and in the former use is also made of the sort of fierce tonal conflict exploited in Beethoven's Waldstein Sonata No. 21 Op. 53 (and before that in No. 16 Op. 31 no. 1). Yet the effect is quite different: with the Hammerklavier we experience an epic challenge while Brahms's harmonic density (two or even four chords to every one of Beethoven's) reduces the gesture to one of stolid vigour; and where his modulations convey physical energy Beethoven's suggest mystery, spiritual exploration. As we might expect, Brahms sometimes draws nearer to Beethoven when there is no overt imitation at all; the passage at the words 'Es zerrinnen meine Qualen' in *Mondenschein* Op. 85 no. 2, for example, reminds one of those moments in Beethoven which Schumann described as '*Abgründe*' (abysses); we are reminded of Beethoven also in *An die Tauben* Op. 63 no. 4, where after verses 1 and 3 have used the same music, verse 5 has a different melody but the same rhythmic distribution. Some of the resemblances (such as that between the general shape of the first movement of Brahms's Horn Trio Op. 40 and that of Beethoven's Piano Sonata No. 22 Op. 54) are probably unconscious, like some of the apparent links between Schubert and Beethoven. For instance, Schubert may well have been unaware of the echoes of Beethoven's Pathétique Sonata, No. 8 Op. 13, in his song *Abendlied der Fürstin* D. 495 or between the Sonata No. 26 Op. 81a *Les Adieux* and *Abschied* D. 957. But when in his *Schicksalslied* Op. 54 Brahms repeats the opening music at the close it is reasonable to suggest that he had in mind Beethoven's Mass in C major Op. 86, where, following the precedent of Mozart's 'Coronation' Mass K. 317, the music of the Kyrie eleison returns as a coda to the whole work in the Dona nobis pacem; certainly he would have been aware of a case like that of *An die ferne Geliebte* Op. 98, where the last song uses material—greatly intensified—from the first.

No matter how much unremitting work his music cost him, Beethoven had an inherent understanding of large-scale form which Brahms (as we might expect from the period of musical history in which he lived) did not. Also Beethoven's was a fundamentally instrumental approach, many of his characteristic fingerprints being obviously instrumental and often pianistic in origin, whereas the influence of the singing voice is apparent in all but the sternest moments of Brahms's symphonies. In a piece such as his Symphony No. 1 Op. 68 we can all too easily sense the relief with which Brahms turned from the dutiful striving of his opening Allegro and Finale to the lyrical expression of the inner movements. Similarly, the third movement of his dour C minor String Quartet Op. 51 no. 1 is essentially lyrical, in no way a Scherzo—and the second movement is a Romanza.

If at the same time he appears reluctant to follow such purely lyrical impulses, never repeating the indulgence represented by the *Magelone Romanzen* Op. 33 or the extroversion of his Paganini Variations Op. 35, this is largely because of the excessive claims made on his behalf by Schumann, and the responsibilities these imposed upon him at so inopportunely early a point in his career. Schumann had previously hailed Mendelssohn in much the same way as a composer who might be expected to reconcile Classic and Romantic outlooks; however, the lack of real conflict in most of Mendelssohn's highly cultivated works made them classicistic rather than either classical or Romantic, and among his imitators this became merely a sentimental academicism. Later it was the same with Brahms's followers. In, say, Parry's oratorio *Job* (greatly admired in its day), we encounter precisely the good intentions and feeble imagination to be expected of late official Victorian art; apart from a Mendelssohnian *The Lord hath Given*, the whole is written in a studiously sub-Brahmsian dialect, replete with self-conscious contrapuntal devices, muddy orchestration and laboured cadences; *When the Morning Stars Sang Together* (from the same work) shows dependence on Brahms at its most inept. A generation later the congested scoring of countless works such as Enescu's Symphony No. 1 shows the situation continuing, though a few items can be found, like Ireland's *Sea Idyll*, where Brahms's influence is more fruitful.

However, like all the other great composers, Brahms had no true successor, because each represents a completion, a fulfilment of certain tendencies which, due to his predilections, opportunities and specific gifts, he draws together out of the musical situation as he finds it. Schumann's view of Brahms as the heir to Beethoven derived from a concept, artificial even within the close-knit musical traditions of Germany, of an apostolic succession of great masters. Hence the youthful Brahms—he was twenty when Schumann's laudatory article appeared in *Die Neue Zeitschrift für Musik*, October 1853—was

45

saddled with the responsibilities of continuing a classical tradition which had much earlier begun to break up—at least so far as it concerned the progressive musical tendencies with which a young man such as Brahms might be expected to sympathize. His difficulties were intensified by the response which Schumann's article—called *Neue Bahnen* (New Paths)—inevitably produced, especially as news of its author's mental deterioration had been spreading for some years. Nor was it to Brahms's advantage that Schumann had earlier lavished praise on such nonentities as Ernst Naumann, Woldemar Bargiel, Ludwig Norman, Julius Schäffer and others. Wilhelm Ambros spoke of the 'morbid exaltation' of *Neue Bahnen*, while Richard Pohl wrote in *Die Neue Zeitschrift* itself, and with good reason, that Brahms should not have been acclaimed as a mature artist on the basis of his earliest works. The composer himself wrote to Schumann that 'The public praise you have lavished on me will have raised public expectation of my achievements so high that I do not know how I am to come up to it.'

So it was that Brahms succumbed to obsessive variation writing and contrapuntal discipline in an attempt to transform his lyricism into something else. (It is interesting to note that Dvořák was later to go through a comparable phase, though for somewhat different reasons, during the years 1875–8, the fruits being his Variations for piano Op. 36, the Symphonic Variations Op. 78 and the variation movements of his String Sextet Op. 48 and Piano Quartet Op. 23.) As noted already, Brahms did succeed in bringing together certain aspects of Baroque, Classical and Romantic music and in many ways his art was richer for the endeavour. Yet lyricism remains his truest and most fundamental expression, embodied in the *Lieder* and some of the keyboard and chamber works. He is comparable to Tennyson, who was set on a false trail by the great success of *In Memoriam* and who then spent too much of his time putting essentially lyrical gifts to work on uncongenial epic ventures. Gounod's career after the success of *Faust* is not dissimilar.

Brahms's concern with the past, his editing and performance of pre-J. S. Bach music, and especially his use of older (pre-Romantic and even pre-classical), techniques has been compared, by amateur psychologists among music commenta-

tors, with Schumann's *'Davidsbund'** or Schubert's cultivation
of a comparatively wide circle of friends as a defence against
the hostile world. In fact, his intensive contrapuntal and
variation-writing studies, even though encouraged by Schumann's claims for him, did accord with his North German
musical background and were, at the same time, part of a
widespread musical tendency at that time.

The search for the German past which had led literary men to
medieval legend in turn led musicians to Bach; more surprisingly, considering the nature of the German tradition, it
led a few of them to Palestrina. The latter could scarcely be
expected to have a permanent effect on German musical
practice, yet his influence is apparent in the *O bone Jesu* Op. 37
no. 1 of Brahms, who was probably led to him by Schumann
(who in turn had met the Palestrina enthusiast Thibaut at
Heidelberg during 1829). Some musicians, such as Mendelssohn who revived Bach's St Matthew Passion (whose last
movement is duly quoted in the Allegretto of Brahms's String
Quintet No. 2 Op. 111), were only affected to a comparatively
superficial degree in their own compositions; these trends did
give rise to some dull, characterless music from Brahms, in
particular his *Ave Maria* Op. 12 and Psalm XIII (not XXIII,
as given in some reference works), as well as to unnecessarily
dry results in pieces such as *Schaffe in mir, Gott* Op. 29 no. 2.
There are several happier instances, though, like the changing
around of parts in *Der Jäger* Op. 22 no. 4 (which should be
compared with *Der englische Jäger*, last of Brahms's so-called *14
Deutsche Volkslieder* that he arranged for SATB and which uses
the same text). Other examples are the *cantus firmus* technique
of the Op. 91 *Lieder* with viola obbligato and the naturally
flowing canon of *Regina coeli* Op. 37 no. 3, or the canon
maintained strictly for sixteen bars with many subsequent
points of imitation in *Warum ist das Licht gegeben?* Op. 74 no. 1;
in this last example Brahms draws a paradoxically Romantic

---

* Another of Schumann's imaginary projections (see footnote, p. 34).
This *Davidsbund* represented an alliance of artists against a confederacy of
philistines. (His piano work Carnaval, Op. 9 ends with a march of the
Davidsbund against the philistines.)

effect well described by Elisabet von Herzogenberg as 'like going into the nave of a great church just as the sun is setting'. Further instances are the canon by inversion of *O Heiland, reiss die Himmel auf* Op. 74 no. 2, the fluent writing, again canonic, of *Beherzigung* Op. 93a no. 6, the antiphonal treatment of *Wenn wir in höchsten Nöten sind* Op. 110 no. 3, and the melody accompanied by a fugue derived from that melody in *Es ist das Heil* Op. 29 no. 1.

These motets of Brahms are quite different from the mere antiquarianism of Grell or Bellermann, whose works really were nothing more than a passive and non-creative response to the revival of interest in Palestrina led by Thibaut and Baini. Similarly, Bruckner's successful combination of sixteenth century influences and the Viennese symphonic tradition in his E minor Mass should not be confused with the stiff-limbed counterpoint of Hummel's masses in D and E flat. (However, in fairness it might be added that Hummel's masses in C, fruitfully influenced by Haydn and perhaps Eybler, and in B flat— which has a fine *Amen* fugue despite Prout's adverse comments —are superior compositions.)

Whether effective or not, Brahms attempted to reconcile strict counterpoint with Romantic expression. An example of this is his *Marienlieder* Op. 22 inspired by the sixteenth-century German secular part-songs of Senfl, Hofheimer and others. These *Marienlieder* should be heard together with such items as Spohr's 1820 Mass—a synthesis of Mozartian chromaticism and sixteenth-century techniques—or the Pastoral and Annunciation of the Angel from Liszt's *Christus*—which again reflects a concern with pre-J. S. Bach music. Examples of later influences paralleling those acting on Brahms are Mendelssohn's organ sonatas Op. 65, which seem more Baroque than nineteenth century, and some of Raff's eclectic works that likewise revive Baroque forms. In such a context Brahms's choice of a passacaglia as finale to his last symphony, albeit with all sorts of motivic interplay and Romantic chordal substitutions, hardly seems exceptional.

Despite all this, he had considerable reservations about the use of older methods, even those of the recent past, saying 'The great Romantics continued sonata form in a lyric spirit which contradicts the inner dramatic nature of the sonata; Schumann himself illustrates this contradiction.' As a lifelong and avid reader, Brahms here might have had in mind the case of Grillparzer, in some ways Germany's greatest poet of the post-Napoleonic period, whose plays lack assurance and power though conscientiously filling the classical moulds. Remembering how much he learnt from Schumann, it is in several respects suprising that, following Beethoven, Brahms's variation sets adhere to strict Baroque form instead of echoing the poetic freedom of Schumann's *Symphonische Etüden* Op. 13. This is particularly suprising since his counterpoint, for all its strictness, also marks a continuation of Schumann's poetic keyboard works in fugal style, such as Op. 72 and his canonic studies for pedal piano, Opp. 56 and 58.

Despite his natural affinity with the German musical past and notwithstanding the mythological references already noted in a few of his *Lieder*, there is nothing in Brahms comparable to the profound feeling for antiquity which informs Berlioz's music (not only in *Les Troyens*). Again, though, one must observe the constant antitheses of Brahms and his sympathy for more conservative composers such as Mendelssohn, whose influence is more frequent than might be expected from their very different modes of expression (even if this is yet another instance of the essential unity of the German musical tradition). Thus Brahms's Capriccio Op. 76 no. 1 has a decidedly Mendelssohnian aspect; *Am Wildbach die Weiden* Op. 44 no. 9 is like one of the older man's barcarolles and both *Der Gärtner* Op. 17 no. 3 and *Die Meere* Op. 20 no. 3 have a distinctly Mendelssohnian suavity.

A relaxation of formal precepts such as occurred early in the Romantic period inevitably leads to uncertainty about structure, and therefore about style as well, particularly when there is a heightened regard for the past and an occasional misuse of its legacy. Brahms's inspiration usually flowed best when unclouded by the complications arising from this regard for the past. However, though a turning away from sonata and symphony was to be expected from the Romantics, contemporary observers in 1860 would have been wrong to assume they were as dead as the trio-sonata or *canzona*, shells not living organisms. During the remainder of the nineteenth century absolute music enjoyed a fresh lease of life even though the forms of symphony and sonata did not dominate instrumental composition as they had at the close of the previous century. Usually—and despite the absurd manifesto against the New German School published in the Berlin *Echo* during 1860 by Brahms, Joachim and a couple of their friends—this entailed no rejection of the aesthetic of Liszt and Wagner, some of the linguistic features of whose music, as we shall see, may be found in Brahms's own music. Also, though Brahms's teacher Marxsen had a detailed knowledge of Beethoven and J. S. Bach that was exceptional for his time, his own pieces also reflect progressive influences such as that of Spohr, as his *Trauerklängen Schleswig-Holsteins* might prove. Spohr's chromaticism equally marks such things as Elizabeth's *Prayer* from Wagner's *Tannhäuser* while his *Jessonda* anticipates aspects of *Tristan*; Schumann demonstrably learnt both from Spohr and Moscheles—a few of whose *Etudes*, such as Op. 70 nos. 5 and 24 and Op. 95 no. 4, anticipate Brahms's keyboard style. It might be added that another item of the latter set, No. 6, resembles a piano transcription of a scene from one of Wagner's operas, while Chopin's Prelude Op. 45 (from bar 13 onwards) also looks forward to Brahms.

Altogether, the separation of music into two camps implicit in the *Echo* statement of 1860 had little reality, a point emphasized by some non-German composers, such as Dvořák who wrote both symphonies and symphonic poems, chamber music and operas. Also, Schumann, despite the important rôle played by his early and extremely Romantic keyboard works in disrupting older forms, had already sought new paths for the sonata idea in such pieces as his Violin Sonatas Opp. 105 and 121, in movements of his String Quartets Op. 41, Piano Trios Opp. 63, 80 and 110 and, using Beethoven as his guide, most noticeably in the Piano Quartet Op. 47. Such endeavours need to be related, especially so far as Brahms is concerned, to the North German symphonic school, for his orchestral music is in fact a synthesis of this and the Viennese tradition. Composers such as Kalliwoda, Volkmann, Dietrich, Bruch and Götz wrote works that if showing no connections with the literary and philosophical aspects of the music of Wagner, Liszt and their immediate associates still absorbed many of their technical procedures. The close resemblances between Bruch's Violin Concerto No. 1 and that of Brahms hardly need stressing, and at the same time the operas of Götz are clearly influenced by the Wagner of *Lohengrin*. Other composers, such as Raff, Ritter, Bronsart and Rheinberger followed Liszt and Wagner more directly yet did not produce music that is substantially different from that of, say, Volkmann. Wagner's heady influence was not always beneficial to such minor talents—as the later songs of Jensen, Brahms's pupil, show. Here natural lyricism is debilitated by harmonic complexities which he was unable to subordinate to proper formal control. Once again, the links between supposedly distinct and even hostile camps become apparent, and it is also plain that Brahms's 'classicism', even though heavily qualified by a Romantic temperament, was not the isolated phenomenon in the music of the latter half of the nineteenth century that it usually is supposed to be.

A similar remark applies to the contrapuntal aspect of his work, for this had roots going further back than the renewed concern with J. S. Bach. Any idea that Brahms's use, in his motets and elsewhere, of the older and more complicated devices of counterpoint marked their revival after a long period of disuse is as false as the similar claim advanced in our own century on Schoenberg's behalf (in connection, for example, with such things as the *Nacht*, *Mondfleck* and *Parodie* movements of his *Pierrot Lunaire* Op. 21 and the choral pieces Opp. 27 and 28). In Schoenberg's case they derived, like certain other features of his style, from Brahms, and in Brahms's from the eighteenth-century *Sturm und Drang* works as well as from late Beethoven.

It is characteristic of German musical traditions that whereas the literary *Sturm und Drang* movement aimed at an overthrow of the *Aufklärung*, in music it resulted in fresh uses for old techniques. In eighteenth-century Vienna, for example, no good composer forgot how to write a fugue, and when in reaction to rococo excesses they wished to give their music stronger fibre, to express greater depth of emotion, they turned naturally to the older contrapuntal methods. This is shown by the insistence on counterpoint in such works as Haydn's Symphony No. 70, by the polyphonic textures of his Piano Sonata in A flat (Hoboken 46)—and notice the prophecy of nineteenth-century tendencies in the Handelian (rather than Bachian) influence on his D major Sonata (Hoboken 37).

Clearer illustrations still are found in the counterpoint of Haydn's Op. 17 String Quartets, intensified in the Op. 20 set; and throughout this period, as the G minor *Sturm und Drang* symphonies of Haydn, Mozart, Koželuch and Vanhal, (all written within a few years of each other) show, counterpoint lived on as a means of controlling and directing emotion, just as it was later used by Brahms.

One might add that some of his rhythmic complexity derives from this period also: for instance such things as the 4/4 phrases over 3/4 bars in the Minuet of Haydn's Symphony No. 65 led eventually to, say, the 3/4+2/4 of the slow movement to Brahms's Piano Trio No. 3 Op. 101 (where the phrases are actually in 7/4, made up of 3+2+2 crotchets). We should also note the effect of pathos achieved in his song *Agnes* Op. 59 no. 5 through the alternation of 2/4 and 3/4, although this, like other Brahmsian devices, perhaps descends more immediately from Marxsen, in particular from the interchange of 3/4 and 4/4 in his Variations on a Peasant Dance Op. 67 no. 1, also found in Brahms's own Variations on a Hungarian Song Op. 21 no. 2.

The balance of old and new in Brahms is an aspect of his striving to reconcile his own Romantic tendencies with a loyalty, instilled by Marxsen and confirmed by Schumann, to the classical past. This drawing together of opposites is reflected by his output as a whole in the way that works of quite different periods refer to one another, early items anticipating late, mature pieces looking back to the composer's beginnings. His *Begräbnisgesang* Op. 13 carries strong foretastes of the Requiem Op. 45 and of the *Vier ernste Gesänge* Op. 121, but it is of rather obvious significance that late or even middle-period works, especially for Brahms's own instrument, the piano, quite often evoke the more expansive music of his youth. Billroth said of the two Rhapsodies Op. 79 that 'In both there is more of the young heaven-storming Johannes than there is in the last works of the mature man'; this is something which, reassuringly, kept breaking out despite the composer's attempts at control. So the D minor Capriccio Op. 116 no. 1 recalls his Ballad in D minor Op. 10 no. 1 and the Intermezzo Op. 117 no. 1 reminds us of the quiet introspection of the piano sonata slow movements. *Kein Haus, keine Heimat* Op. 94 no. 5 also looks back to the brusqueness of his early works, and there is a close resemblance, surely curious in the circumstances, between the final vocal phrase of the last of his *Vier ernste Gesänge* Op. 121 and *Wie bist du, meine Königin* Op. 32 no. 9— the latter being a gay song in contrast to the seriousness of Op. 121.

It was Brahms's misfortune that he worked in a musical world divided by Wagner, the emphases of which were such that his concentration on traditional forms of instrumental composition was interpreted in many quarters as a tediously correct academicism. Conveniently it was forgotten that following the first unsuccessful public performances of his Piano Concerto No. 1 Op. 15 in 1859 at Hanover and Leipzig it was only Liszt's Weimar party who had anything good to say for the composer or his music at all; the classicists of Leipzig and other conservatives wholly condemned the work, one respected journal calling it a 'wilderness of screaming dissonances and discordant sounds'.

A true understanding of Brahms's contribution was, indeed, always clouded by factionalist disputes, which produced a simplified view both of the elements of his music and of his relationships with his contemporaries. Such controversies are now history but their exaggerations long remained influential, both in respect of the wild claims made on Brahms's behalf and the reactions these inevitably produced. The Wagner versus Brahms dispute was simply a new version of the earlier, and happily less prolonged one of those who wished to set Mendelssohn against Schumann. It was largely the creation of propagandists who, ignoring the essentially lyrical nature of Brahms's gifts, tried to put him on the same level as Bach and Beethoven—a strategem which Brahms, as several of his letters show, had the good sense angrily to repudiate. Even so, Hadow wrote of Brahmsian fugal movements that 'succeed where Beethoven has failed' and could say of the second movement to the Requiem Op. 45 that 'To find a defect here is to criticise our own judgement'. And according to Fuller-Maitland, '*All* the themes of Brahms have the *finest* melodic curves that were *ever* devised in music' (italics added). In such a context, the asinine comment of Bernard Shaw (a supporter of the Wagner faction) on the 'mere brute musical faculty' of the Requiem and *Schicksalslied* Op. 54 seems almost excusable, though Brahms, like one of his musical descendants,

Schoenberg, suffered more from his friends than from his enemies.

In certain of Brahms's works a struggle is evident between Viennese classical and New German (Lisztian and Wagnerian) tendencies, just as in Dvořák, where it is complicated by a genuine nationalism very different from the pseudo-Hungarian style that Brahms grafted on to some of his music and which will be discussed later. Wagner systematically used the *Leitmotiv*, every idea, person, object or event having its own motive or theme; though related to the Lieder composers' tradition of word-painting, it is something with which Brahms was never directly associated. However, this must be balanced with his striking use of a motto theme, subject to various transformations, in the Symphony No. 3 Op. 90 (whose first movement includes a passage, just before the second subject appears, strongly reminiscent in melody and harmony of the *Tannhäuser* Venusberg music). Again, though Brahms composed no symphonic poems, some of his keyboard pieces, like certain of Liszt's, are prefixed with quotations from Romantic poetry whose atmosphere and mood are closely reflected in the music. Such items as the Andante espressivo of his Sonata No. 3 Op. 5 or the Ballad Op. 10 no. 1. known, as stated above, to be based on Herder's translation of the *Edward* ballad, are songs without words, almost programmatic, especially in the latter case; and it is no use pretending this was merely a youthful indiscretion, as the Intermezzo Op. 117 no. 1 will prove.

Linking such things to the manifesto against the New German School mentioned on p. 50, one might say that while normally dissenters who take the field against a prevailing outlook are more convincing in their polemics than in their art, the opposite is true of Brahms—and of Joachim, whose Violin Concerto (and even more his *Frühlingsphantasie*) show the obvious influence of Liszt. Brahms's work persistently suggests that what he actually opposed was not the musical endeavours of Wagner and Liszt so much as their literary and philosophical orientation, these being matters which, though he was not really clear on the question, he felt strongly should not be mixed up with music. Besides Wagner's admiration for Brahms's Handel Variations Op. 24 (which was expressed about as positively as he could bring himself to express admiration for the work of a composer who was not safely dead), we should recall that Brahms rarely missed a Wagner performance in Vienna and always regretted his decision, characteristic though it was, not to visit Bayreuth. As late as 1882 he wrote to Bülow, 'I need hardly say that I go in dread of the Wagnerians, who would spoil my pleasure in the best of Wagner.' Brahms also called himself 'The best of Wagnerites' and said to Widmann that his comprehension of Wagner's scores was probably more complete than that of any contemporary. Certainly Wolf's complaint that 'Brahms writes symphonies regardless of what has happened to music in the meantime' is wide of the mark so far as the symphonies (or any other part of his output) is concerned. This is shown by many definite resemblances between his and Wagner's work.

Indeed, there could be no clearer indication of the affinities linking their allegedly so different musical languages than the fact that some of Brahms's 'Wagnerian moments' actually anticipate the operatic scores of which they remind us, and sometimes by many years. Thus the horn signal which opens *Es tönt ein voller Harfenklang* Op. 17 no. 1 (1860), besides resembling a similar passage in the finale to Chopin's F minor Piano Concerto Op. 21 (1829–30), looks forward to the opening of Act II of *Tristan* (1865); the contrapuntal combination of themes starting at bar 162 of the opening movement of Brahms's Piano Sonata No. 2 Op. 2 (1852) should be compared with that in the overture to *Die Meistersinger* (1868), while the *Begräbnisgesang* Op. 13 (circa 1858), as well as having links, noted above, with the Requiem Op. 45 (1857–68) and *Vier ernste Gesänge* Op. 121 (1896), has a similar atmosphere to the procession of Titurel's body in *Parsifal* Act III (1882). Sometimes a Brahms score looks both backwards and forwards, as when the A flat theme of the Op. 5 Piano Sonata echoes Elsa's Dream from *Lohengrin* while the chief phrase of the conclusion to the slow movement looks ahead to Sachs' '*Dem Vogel, der heut' sang*' in *Die Meistersinger*. And there are two quotations, presumably unconscious, from *Der Ring des Nibelungen* in the outer movements of Brahms's String Quartet No. 1 Op. 51 no. 1.

Anticipations may be found, in less specific form, elsewhere and still earlier, of course, as in the highly Wagnerian move from E flat to B major in Schubert's *Am See* D. 746 (1822–3), and the point is in a way confirmed by *Sind es Schmerzen, sind es*

Freuden, No. 3 of Brahms's *Magelone Romanzen* Op. 33, which in turn combines an allusion to Schubert's *Ganymed* D. 544 at the words 'Liebe, den heiligen Schwur' with one to *Tristan* at 'bleib ich ihr ferne, sterb ich gerne'—with, for good measure, a reference to Schumann at the word 'Hoffnung'. Again, in *Wie soll ich die Freude, die Wonne denn tragen*, sixth of the *Magelone Romanzen*, while the rhythmic layout of the *poco sostenuto* passage recalls the middle section of Brahms's Ballad Op. 10 no. 4, the harmony seems influenced by that of *Tristan* and *Das Rheingold*. Similarly, the *Tristan* love theme appears in disguised form in the central part of *Sehnsucht* Op. 112 no. 1; finally there is an affinity, definite yet harder to isolate, between 'O sink' hernieder' from *Tristan* and Brahms's *Der Tod, das ist die kühle Nacht* Op. 96 no. 1.

As this obvious sympathy with, and detailed knowledge of, Wagner's work might suggest, Brahms did for many years seriously consider writing an opera himself. This is minimized and even hastily dismissed in most of the literature about the composer, chiefly on the basis of a single letter written during 1882 to the wife of Franz Wüllner, in which he speaks of the difficulties attendant upon theatrical work. But in 1870 he had written to Clara Schumann that 'Wagner would not in the least deter me from tackling an opera with the greatest enthusiasm. . . . On my long list of wishes such an opera ranks even higher than the position of music director.' The cantata *Rinaldo* Op. 50 (which may interestingly be compared with Bruch's *Odysseus* Op. 41) is as near as he ever got to this. Writing to his publisher Simrock after its première he was under no illusion about its reception by press and public. However, he did vehemently defend it against several friends, such as Billroth, who found Goethe's text 'repulsive'. (Perhaps it is too dependent on Tasso's *Gerusalemme Liberata*.)

An opera was a less unlikely venture for a German composer of that time than some writers on Brahms have assumed: Goslich, in his *Beiträge zur Geschichte der Deutschen Romantischen Oper* (Leipzig, 1937), lists around 100 German opera companies between 1800 and Wagner's later period, and this is confirmed by the more immediately contemporary record of Paldamus's *Das Deutsche Theater der Gegenwart* (Mainz, 1857), which tells us that in 1857, during Brahms's youth, there were about 100 municipal and other permanent organizations performing opera, approximately seventy travelling companies and twenty-three court operas.

Opera in Germany (though to a lesser extent than France) was a battlefield of aesthetic and social currents of exactly the sort which Brahms would tend to avoid, yet Widmann's *Brahms in Erinnerungen* (Berlin, 1898) leaves no doubt of his seriousness over the project. Widmann was the librettist of the once highly successful *Der Widerspänstigen Zähmung* (1874) by Götz (to whose *Nänie* Brahms's work of the same name, Op. 82, bears considerable resemblance); he tells us the composer mentioned Gozzi's *König Hirsch* and *Der Rabe* as possible starting points and also *Das laute Geheimnis*, though in Gozzi's theatrically more effective version, not the Calderon original which he considered too stiff. Widmann also remarks on Brahms's keen interest in theatrical matters, saying that 'Being possessed of extraordinary dramatic instinct, it gave him much pleasure to analyse any scheme for a dramatic work'. The problem of finding the right libretto was very far from being unique to Brahms, and even before meeting Widmann he had given careful consideration to a couple of his plays—*Der geraubte Schleier* and *Iphigenia in Delphi*—as well as to Schiller's *Demetrius* and later to Kleist's *Käthchen von Heilbronn*. His interest in such fully worked-out dramas is explained by his belief that music, far from being continuous, should be linked by spoken dialogue, as in the eighteenth-century German *Singspiel*. By reserving music for the more intense moments, he felt the two arts would be able to assert their full claims while still enhancing each other at key points. Not quite incidentally, Dietrich tells us that the composer 'Had a deep-rooted dislike of all displays of solemnity', and the idea of an opera undoubtedly appealed to the highly emotional side of his nature. Perhaps it appealed too much and he grew even more than usually cautious. But he continued returning to the matter, corresponding with Widmann even as late as 1888 about *Das laute Geheimnis* and *König Hirsch*.

It ought not to be assumed that if Brahms had written an opera it would necessarily have turned out at all like Schumann's *Genoveva*; indeed, he would probably have done much better than Schubert (*Fierrabras* being his only stage work with

57

any dramatic spirit). Examples of operatic affinities (both Wagnerian and otherwise) in Brahms's *Lieder* have already been given, but a few more can be added, such as *Heimkehr* Op. 7 no. 6, the oldest of his surviving songs. Here the material is insufficiently developed for the content of the piece, yet the expression, particularly at the start, is quasi-operatic—a move towards the elaborated *scenas* of the *Magelone Romanzen* Op. 33. Notice also the sustained dramatic tension of the Op. 75 Ballads and Romances (though the first three need to be done with considerable freedom to make their full effect), and the comparable impact of *Willst du, dass ich geh?* Op. 71 no. 4, with its passionate climax. *Verrat* Op. 105 no. 5, however, should be recognized as an uneasy attempt at melodrama which, despite its varied treatment of the middle section, does not succeed.

Rarely in opera, Wagnerian or otherwise, can we expect to find the intimate communing of Brahms's chamber music, keyboard pieces Opp. 116–19 and many of his *Lieder*. Yet this quality is matched in the subtle expression of some of Liszt's piano works, several of whose pieces, such as *Paysage*, No. 3 of his *Études d'exécution transcendante*, the Paganini Etude No. 6 or his transcription of Wagner's *Tannhäuser* overture, anticipate various aspects of Brahms's keyboard style. This is not especially surprising if we consider the Lisztian bravura which opens and closes the finale of Brahms's Piano Sonata No. 2 Op. 2, many of his own Paganini Variations Op. 35— or the reconciliation of Brahmsian and Lisztian tendencies achieved in a work such as Richard Strauss's *Burleske*.

There are many instances of Lisztian transformation of themes throughout Brahms's production. However, we might expect this from one who, particularly outside his variation sets, contributed so much to the technique of variation. Of course the principle of thematic transformation did not begin with Liszt, nor with Schubert (e.g. the 'Wanderer' Fantasy D. 760) from whom Liszt is supposed to have taken the idea, but goes back to the medieval masses based on plainsong and folk melodies. A subsequent instance may be found by comparing the Kyrie and Sanctus of Palestrina's *Assumpta est Maria* of 1593. The procedure took on dramatic significance during the nineteenth century, not only in Wagner's thoroughgoing use of the *Leitmotiv* but with the more primitive devices of the same kind found, among other places, in Dvořák's operas, which had descended from Spohr, Weber and even Marschner.

A peculiarly sanctimonious air is assumed by almost the entire Brahms literature when discussing his relationship, musical and otherwise, with Liszt. For instance, the apocryphal tale of Brahms falling asleep as Liszt played his B minor Sonata is always joyously cited as incontrovertible evidence of the shallowness of that great work; yet the sole authority for this incident is Reményi, the violinist with whom Brahms was touring, and in the next breath we are usually told that Reményi (an adherent of Liszt's) was extremely unreliable! Assurance is also normally given that the Lisztian thematic transformations to be found in Brahms's early works were a youthful indiscretion, a demon he soon cast out. But this is completely untrue, for just as the opening theme of the finale to his Piano Sonata No. 1 Op. 1 (1852–3) derives from that of the first movement (or vice versa):

so the second theme of the Intermezzo Op. 117 no. 2 (1892) is a transformation of the first:

Note also how the opening gesture of the Piano Sonata No. 3 Op. 5 is changed:

or how in the finale of the same work the subsidiary D flat theme gradually claims attention with a diminution of time values and an increase of tempo until it is transformed from a dignified, chorale-like melody into material for a brilliant coda:

And compare this with the relation between the introduction of Brahms's Clarinet Quintet Op. 115 (1891) and the theme of its Presto movement:

Further examples can easily be found: in the C minor String Quartet Op. 51 no. 1 in the links between the openings of the first movement, Romanza and Finale; in the third movement to his Symphony No. 2 Op. 73, where both Presto sections derive from the Allegretto material; in the Intermezzo Op. 119 no. 2, where the Andante grazioso theme is a transformation of that of the outer sections; or in the song *Die Schnur, die Perl an Perle* Op. 57 no. 7, where the theme is used almost throughout, with many expressive modifications.

There were numerous criticisms of these Lisztian transformations. Hanslick, most vociferous and almost the least perceptive of Brahms's partisans, called them 'a monstrous anti-musical procedure'; the 1860 manifesto said they were 'contrary to the innermost spirit of music, strongly to be deplored and condemned'; and in his letters Brahms repeatedly uses the term 'swindle' when referring to Liszt's music. If these criticisms had any foundation, it is rather hard to explain, let alone explain away, Brahms's frequent use of the device throughout his career. Without resorting to impertinent psychological guesswork, one may perhaps suggest that the aggression covered a sense of indebtedness, and that Brahms's feelings were, as so often, ambivalent is confirmed by his remark to Arthur Friedheim (quoted in Herbert Westerby's *Liszt and his Piano Works*, London, 1936) that the operatic fantasies, the very last part of Liszt's output we might expect him to admire, 'represent the classicism of the piano'. In the end there seems little point in trying to make sense of the anti-Lisztian comments of Brahms and his friends. It is true, however, that he was never on good personal terms with many of his creative equals, with Wagner, Liszt and still less with younger men such as Wolf; Schumann was the only great composer to whom he was close, and this must be taken into account when studying his spoken or written statements, even on the technique of composition. He tried, via contrapuntal complexities and variation writing, to discipline some of the youthful passion out of his music, the *Magelone Romanzen* and Paganini Variations, Opp. 33 and 35, being intended as fare-wells, happily incomplete, to a part of himself. Similarly Liszt, as we may observe by comparing the original and the neater, more conventional revised versions of his *Études d'exécution transcendante*, for example, sometimes repressed the fire and Romantic exuberance of his initial discoveries. Luckily he did not always succeed; but the fact that Brahms and Liszt sometimes made the same mistake is a link between them which goes beyond the details of their music.

Another link, however, is the restraint and economy that, despite a few exceptions like the Op. 101 Piano Trio, mark nearly all Brahms's late scores and which find a parallel, though a markedly ascetic one, in Liszt's sombre final piano works. If anything, Brahms's late pieces are more rather than less sensuous in sound and texture; this is because during his closing years he became a composer of elegiac disillusionment, as a few of his early *Lieder*—such as *An eine Äolsharfe* Op. 19 no. 5—had long before prophesied. As such, he leads us, with his consolatory yet pessimistic musings, to our own century and to the dark and mysterious shadows of Mahler.

Yet it is never merely a question of his tone of voice, for Brahms's subtly balanced asymmetries of phrase-length, his cross-rhythms, counterpoints within the figuration (derived from Schumann), laid foundations for Reger and Schoenberg as well as for Mahler, just as surely as Wagner's did when he dissolved the old formal patterns of opera into a continuous dramatic whole. Another link with Mahler and Schoenberg (and with Liszt also) is in the hints of what may be termed a chamber-music way of writing for the orchestra (with separate lines rather than masses) which occurs in such Brahms songs as *Spanisches Lied* Op. 6 no. 1, with its violin-like accompanimental phrases and delicate evocation of a village band, *Heimkehr* Op. 7 no. 6 and *Wie soll ich die Freude, die Wonne denn tragen* Op. 33 no. 6 with their suggestions of the cello, or the part-song *Verlorene Jugend* Op. 104 no. 4, that Elisabet von Herzogenberg referred to as 'the little string quartet'. The kind of orchestral approach implied here, or at the beginning of *Sind es Schmerzen, sind es Freuden* Op. 33 no. 3, which seems to demand clarinets and harp over double bass pizzicato, is usually regarded as Mahler's innovation, though really it goes back beyond the exquisite *Gretchen* movement of Liszt's Faust Symphony to Mozart's Symphony K. 318. (One might add that an earlier case of the *Lied*, Loewe's *Die naechtliche Heerschau*, with its trills and fanfares, anticipates another quite different aspect of Mahler—his grotesque echoes of military music, perhaps via the martial overtones of Brahms's *Keinen hat es noch gereut* Op. 33 no. 1.)

A number of other features in Brahms's work, all contradicting the settled view of him as the nineteenth century's great reactionary classicist, should be mentioned, such as his use of what is known as 'progressive tonality'. A score like Mahler's *Lieder eines fahrenden Gesellen* (1883) starts in D minor, passes through F sharp minor, B major and E minor to close in a remote F minor; this was anticipated on a smaller scale by a Brahms *Lied* such as *Von waldbekränzter Höhe* Op. 57 no. 1 (circa 1868), which is interestingly organized in fourteen-bar sections, nearly all different, the second beginning in D minor and ending in B flat major, the third commencing in B flat major and closing in B minor, and so on. Simpler cases are *Abendregen* Op. 70 no. 4, which opens in A minor and finishes in a C major associated with the rainbow of Keller's poem, or *Vom Strande* Op. 69 no. 6, which although in A minor begins in F major. As so often with the German tradition, this is a development which matured slowly and one should remember examples like Mozart's G minor Piano Quartet K. 478, whose movements are respectively in G minor, B flat and G major, besides *Lieder* such as Schubert's *Totengräber-Weise* D. 869, whose first vocal sentence starts in F sharp minor, passes via D major to a cadence in E minor then recommences in C major and goes through F and G major to end in D major—all in eight bars.

Other Schubert songs, like *Nähe des Geliebten* D. 162, *An den Schlaf* D. 447 or *Jägers Abendlied* D. 368, that make their points very quickly, likewise point to the increasing amount of tautly structured music, and this was, of course, carried forward by Brahms. For him, this development, with its inevitable consequence of minimal exact repetition noticeable in such *Lieder* as his *Der Tod, das ist die kühle Nacht* Op. 96 no. 1, stemmed from Beethoven rather than Schubert; the models were not merely the obvious ones like the Bagatelles Opp. 119 and 126, but the Op. 95 String Quartet, the Piano Sonatas Opp. 90 and 101, and overtures such as Coriolanus and Egmont, which summarize the whole drama in a few minutes.

The tendency towards brevity recurs throughout Brahms's work from *Marias Kirchgang* Op. 22 no. 2 to *Kein Haus, keine Heimat* Op. 94 no. 5, and points directly to the concentration of Webern and of many Schoenberg pieces—as in its way does the unusually spare accompaniment to *Lerchengesang* Op. 70 no. 2. A further case is *Junge Lieder* Op. 63 no. 5, an exuberant song which, although it gives the impression of having been conceived in one breath (like *O komm, holde Sommernacht* Op. 58 no. 4), is set so that no two lines are exactly the same: the first is sung once to a four-bar phrase, the second twice to a pair of two-bar phrases, the third once to a two-bar, the fourth twice —once to a two- and once to a four-bar phrase. Note also the compression of *In meiner Nächte Sehnen* Op. 57 no. 5, the middle pair of whose four verses are set as one piece, the first verse being of eleven bars, the second and third of nineteen and the fourth again of eleven. The contrapuntal references to the theme in the bass during this latter song are an aid to unity, of course, and such devices are taken much further in, say, the third movement of Brahms's A minor String Quartet Op. 51 no. 2 with its multiple canons which point towards Webern. Similarly, the predominating fourths of this passage from the last movement of the Piano Quartet No. 2 Op. 26,

63

while looking back to such moments as this in Mozart (the relationship of whose keyboard Gigue K. 574 to the Gigue of Schoenberg's Suite Op. 25 should be carefully examined),

also anticipate certain constructions in Schoenberg's Chamber Symphony No. 1 Op. 9 and in Berg's Piano Sonata Op. 1. A comparable passage on a bass of rising fourths in the finale to Brahms's Symphony No. 4 Op. 98 more directly prefigures a passage in Berg's Chamber Concerto:

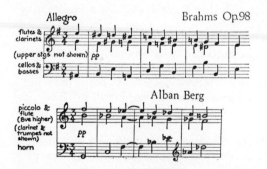

Both these basses should be compared with the main subject of the Schoenberg Chamber Symphony No. 1 (bars 5–7). Again, in this melody from the Allegretto of Brahms's Symphony

No. 1 Op. 68 the mirror inversion of the first half by the second anticipates the retrogrades and inversions of serial technique:

Von ewiger Liebe Op. 43 no. 1, incorrectly described as a folk-song setting in more than one reference work, is also relevant here, being in three parts each with its own material, and with no repeats; this is justified by Wenzig's poem, and the song is an early instance (circa 1868) of a text lending continuity to a work in the way associated with the atonal settings of Schoenberg and Webern. A less direct instance is the Ballad Op. 10 no. 1; its three companion pieces, Nos. 2–4, are decidedly imperfect wholes, but No. 1, with its oppressive atmosphere and carefully varied phrase-lengths, is successful, partly at least through so closely following Herder's translation of the Scots ballad *Edward* and deriving coherence from it. The *Lied* in general anticipates composers like Webern and Schoenberg through its recitative element which led to the *Sprechgesang* of such works as *Pierrot Lunaire,* and other traditions occasionally pointed in that direction too, as when Verdi directed his singers in *Macbeth* to speak rather than sing their lines.

The drive to make Brahms seem as austerely Classical a figure as possible, reflected in so much of the literature devoted to him, was part of a very protracted reaction against Romanticism which has now run its course. His early description of himself as 'Johannes Kreisler Junior', after E. T. A. Hoffman's character, and his collection of favourite extracts from Romantic literature into a private anthology which he called '*Des jungen Kreislers Schätzkastlein*' suggest Brahms's own initial feelings on the matter. This is reinforced by the dedication of his first set of *Lieder,* Op. 3, to Bettina von Arnim; this lady, sister of Clemens Brentano and wife of Achim von Arnim, was a close friend of Goethe and Beethoven, and was among the leading female representatives of the German Romantic movement. One might also recall such rather unascetic traits as Brahms's love of Italy, to which he made eight lengthy visits, his admiration for Bizet's *Carmen* and the Verdi Requiem. Equally to the point are Joachim's description of Brahms's playing when they first met in 1853 as 'So tender, so full of fancy, so free, so fiery'—and the fact that at his initial public appearance in Hamburg he included Thalberg's Norma Fantasy Op. 12 in his programme!

A further sign of Romantic temperament is Brahms's comment in an 1867 letter to Albert Dietrich that 'It's not much use my making plans as I only do what the spirit moves me to', though Billroth could see a Faust-like struggle for perfection in the first movement of the Symphony No. 1 Op. 68, describing it in a letter to Hanslick as 'A kind of Faustian overture'. Brahms's collection of old books and musical manuscripts expressed an essentially Romantic desire to preserve the past, and even Nietzsche understood how deeply rooted was his nostalgia, writing in his essay *Der Fall Wagner*: 'If we discount what he imitates, what he borrows from the great old or exotic modern styles, what remains as his most personal is his longing.' (This is perhaps the place to comment on Nietzsche's dismissal of Brahms, on another occasion, with the oft-quoted phrase, 'His is the melancholy of impotence'. This occurs in a letter of 1888 during which, as in the essay just mentioned, he rends his former idol, Wagner. Nietzsche goes on to say that Peter Gast is the only person left who is writing good music, and, presumably to justify this, he winds up with an attack on Brahms. He was not unaffected by the fact that both Wagner and Brahms had made it clear that they did not like his own musical compositions; what Gast thought of them is not known.)

The Romantic aspect of even the most conscientiously planned of Brahms's works did not pass unnoticed. The Andante to his Symphony No. 4 Op. 98 evoked for the young Richard Strauss 'A funeral procession moving in silence across moonlit heights', and Billroth thought the Symphony No. 2 Op. 73 was 'Like blue heavens, the murmur of brooks, sunshine and cool green shadow'. The sombre forest scene of a song like *Jägerlied* Op. 66 no. 4 inevitably gave rise to similar responses, Elisabet von Herzogenberg comparing *Sommerabend* Op. 84 no. 1 to an engraving by C. W. Dietrich, the eighteenth-century German painter and etcher; for Hanslick, *Geheimnis* Op. 71 no. 3 had 'The most exquisite scent of lilies in the moonlight' and Kalbeck described *Ständchen* Op. 106 no. 1 as 'a moonlight nocturne *à la* Spitzweg'. Yet while it was reasonable enough for Clara Schumann to call the Paganini Variations Op. 35 '*Hexen-Variationen*', surely Joachim was going too far in seeing the problems of Hero and Leander portrayed in the finale to the Symphony No. 3 Op. 90, as was Kalbeck in glimpsing the temptations of St Anthony in the Variations Op. 56! Still, it was with unusual explicitness that Brahms referred in several letters to the way his Piano Quartet No. 3 Op. 60 enshrined 'The Wertherian moods of my Düsseldorf years', and we might, for contrast, note the hunting rhythms of the Scherzo and Finale to his Horn Trio Op. 40 or in *Lieder* such as *Parole* Op. 7 no. 2, the suggestion of bells in the part-song *Marias Kirchgang* Op. 22 no. 2, the sheer light-heartedness of his duet *Der Jäger und sein Liebchen* Op. 28 no. 4, or of the *Rondo alla Zingarese* in his Piano Quartet No. 1 Op. 25. And despite the heading to the slow movement of Mozart's Piano Concerto K. 466 (Romanza) there is nothing in the least classical about Brahms's use of titles such as Romanza (Op. 118 no. 5) or *Notturno* (*O schöne Nacht* Op. 92 no. 1), though his production of a *Gondellied*, in *Auf dem See* Op. 59 no. 2, quite independent of the Mendelssohnian model deserves attention. Considering Brahms's admiration for Johann Strauss the younger and his encouragement of Lehár, Hanslick's air of awestruck speechlessness at his composition of waltzes was quite inappropriate ('Brahms and waltzes! The two words stare at each other in positive amazement . . .'). This point is underlined by the mischievous quotation of a waltz by Gung'l in *Minnelied* Op. 71 no. 5 and, less directly, by the reference in *Wie froh und frisch mein Sinn sich hebt* Op. 33 no. 14, at 'In lieber, dämmernder Ferne', to a military march popular in Hamburg during Brahms's youth.

Romantic also, in their way, are the signs of the influence of Chopin's formal innovations on certain of Brahms's sonata movements. And there is a link between the scene-painting of *Unbewegte laue Luft* Op. 57 no. 8, with its evocation of a sultry, rather oppressive summer night, the gentle fountain noises of *Serenade* Op. 58 no. 8 or the bird-like phrases of *Vögelein durchrauscht die Luft* Op. 52 no. 13 and Brahms's acute yet still

67

partly unrecognized sense of colour and texture with all vocal and instrumental combinations.

Any division between 'thought' and 'colour' here is a puritanical delusion of the sort to which certain aspects of the German musical tradition all too often give rise, yet it is extraordinary that Brahms's alleged indifference to sensuous appeal has so often been advanced as if it were a point in his favour. The fact that a number of his scores were cast and recast for several media in turn—instances being the Piano Concerto No. 1 Op. 15 and the Piano Quintet Op. 34—far from showing that he was loftily unconcerned over matters of texture and colour quite obviously proves the exact opposite. Brahms's main compositional aim with his *Liebeslieder* Waltzes Opp. 52 and 65, for example, was to transfer the waltz-idea to an unfamiliar medium, to add new colours, even if Schumann's *Spanische Liebeslieder* Op. 138 did provide a model. And in the keyboard pieces Opp. 116–19 a wide range of moods is suggested by fresh piano textures alone. If anything it is Liszt, in such late works as *Czárdás macabre* or *Am Grabe Richard Wagners*, who shows himself austerely indifferent to tone-colour—while Brahms basks in the benign mellow light of his clarinet pieces Opp. 114, 115 and 120. Extreme care over orchestration is apparent in the manuscript of his Symphony No. 3 Op. 90, much of the effect of his Horn Trio Op. 40 is lost if the horn is barbarously replaced with a cello and the Sonatas Op. 120 are never well served by the clarinet's usurpation by a viola.

Further instances of his sensitivity in such matters abound, such as the exquisite combinations of light tones in the choral songs with horns and harp Op. 17 and of dark tones in the two *Lieder* for contralto Op. 91, with their brooding viola obbligatos—in each case the voices and instruments offering different shades of the same emotion; of *Gestillte Sehnsucht* Op. 91 no. 1 it might be said that Rückert's opening line, '*In gold'nen Abendschein getauchet, wie feierlich die Wälder steh'n*'* is itself a perfect description of the music. Again, much has been made of Brahms's marvellous restraint in not using trombones in any of his concertos, yet consider how effectively he writes for them in the Requiem Op. 45. Another choral work, his

---

* 'Bathed in golden light of evening, how festively the woods stand.'

Triumphlied Op. 55, was described as 'A glistening mass of colour', and though in this case it is very easy to disagree with so favourable a comment, we should note the interesting mixture of tones in the Rhapsody Op. 53, with its contralto soloist, male voice choir and orchestra. Another interesting invention is in *Die bucklichte Fiedler* Op. 93a no. 1, where the voices imitate the tuning of a violin at the start of the waltz section. Indeed, provided we are not dealing with undesirable substitutions of instruments in his chamber works such as Opp. 40 or 120, Brahms's final choice of medium nearly always seems perfect, especially in chamber and vocal forms, the six-part choir of his *Gesang der Parzen* Op. 89 being an apt though unobtrusive example.

Very many of Brahms's *Lieder* and other pieces such as the keyboard works Opp. 116–19 are in ternary, ABA, form without any reference to sonata form, and even in a score like the Clarinet Quintet Op. 115, which does keep to the outlines of sonata style, there are many links with Baroque variational procedure (similarly, the *Vier ernste Gesänge* Op. 121 look back to the Baroque cantata). The sonata principle, then, was not the be-all and end-all for him, as has been claimed, and this again is what might be expected from the lyrical nature of his gifts. At the same time, there is virtually nothing in Brahms's music, even in the earliest *Lieder*, such as *Liebestreu* Op. 3 no. 1, or in the piano Scherzo Op. 4, which is improvisatory, as Schumann, especially in his songs, often is; Brahms is less apparently intuitive, more consciously systematic. The rare consistency of his output is, of course, the result of his readiness to spend an exceptional amount of time over even the smallest pieces, returning to them repeatedly, sometimes at intervals of several years. For this reason opus numbers are only a rough guide to chronology, the two motets of Op. 74, for example, being written a decade apart. Concerning this protracted work, Brahms said to Jenner, during a lesson, 'Only a few can have found it as hard as I have', and writing of Bach, Mozart and Schubert, in a letter to Simrock, he says, 'If we can't imitate them in composing beautifully, we should at least avoid matching their speed of composing.'

Possibly due to this, Brahms was spared some of the errors of taste into which earlier and later Romantic composers fell, especially in their attitudes to older music. He produced nothing, for example, that is remotely comparable to Moscheles' cello obbligatos to some of the Preludes of *Das Wohltemperierte Klavier*, or Schumann's keyboard accompaniments to solo violin works by Paganini and Bach, Grieg's second piano parts to Mozart's keyboard sonatas, or MacDowell's reharmonization of the Anna Magdalena Notebook. Indeed, Brahms's method of composition was such that each element had a chance of influencing the rest. This was not invariably fruitful, as can be seen from a case such as the duet *Weg der Liebe* Op. 20 no. 1, where the canonic writing at the start of the second verse inhibits the lyricism, this being compounded by a rather too conventional accompaniment. But usually extremes, instead of being in any way avoided, were cultivated and reconciled, the whole fabric of his music being essentially progressive. (The fact that Brahms, like other great composers, could work in this manner, on several different levels of intensity at once, is confirmed by his being simultaneously occupied with the daemonic Piano Concerto No. 1 Op. 15 and his genial String Sextet No. 1 Op. 18.) A great artist's drive towards individual utterance always produces its own personal methods whose sole aim is to provide an unambiguous vehicle for his thinking. Though created by his own immediate need for expression, such a technique usually contains, as Brahms's certainly does, hints of the future development of musical shapes into more plastic musical thought.

Although a product of a very different tradition, it is significant that Berlioz, the first genuinely neo-classical composer, was for many decades rejected while Brahms quickly won acceptance. This was because although the latter's large-scale forms inclined towards classicism, his melody, harmony, and above all the temperament these communicate were altogether Romantic. It is always possible to find parallels between contemporaries and these are partly due to what can only be called the *Zeitgeist*, and more specifically to the common practice of the time, but these admitted relationships tell us a limited amount about an individual score. Thus, although one cannot deny the links between Wagner and Brahms, and these are a useful indication of the latter's progressive sympathies, it is more important that these two composers produced different results—even if many of them were later drawn together by Schoenberg. This point is emphasized by the obvious fact that while the music of both Brahms and Berlioz displays a remarkable and still partly unrecognized rhythmic invention, not least in the use of cross-rhythms, again the results led along very different paths. Actually, comparison between Brahms and another French composer, Saint-Saëns (who was born in 1835 and thus was an almost exact contemporary), shows how subjective the former's Romanticism was. For example, in Saint-Saëns's Symphony No. 3 Op. 78 of 1886 we find many Romantic devices, such as Lisztian thematic transformation and counterpoint used with the fluency of Brahms near his best, yet they are all synthesized in a way that robs them of some of their essential point, this being a weakness that Brahms was usually able to avoid. An instance nearer home is Richard Strauss's *Mein Auge* Op. 37 no. 4, a setting of a Dehmel love poem which most oddly brings together, yet does not reconcile, early Romantic fulfilment and late—almost belated—Romantic regret.

In the end it was the uncompromising balance of diverse, even contradictory, qualities that Brahms achieves at his finest which gives his music its basic character. Yet as our knowledge of his output grows we may come to agree with Geiringer that Brahms, not only in his closing years but whenever he could, 'Reverted to the chamber music, the piano works and the songs of his youth', rather as the final canvas Gauguin painted in Tahiti was a Breton landscape and as Berlioz at last returned to Gluck with *Les Troyens*.

Unlike various *Lieder* by Schumann where the voice, it seems, can add little to what the piano is eloquently telling us, Brahms's songs have a unity of voice and keyboard, each giving a new and vital dimension to the other. That their expression is fully achieved—which could hardly be claimed for the Strauss example noted above—is emphasized by songs like *Phänomen* Op. 61 no. 3, which, like *O komm, holde Sommernacht* Op. 58 no. 4 or *Junge Lieder* Op. 63 no. 5 already mentioned in this regard, seem the result of a single, and complete, moment of inspiration. In fact, partly through his patience and craftsmanlike persistence, Brahms managed to maintain a remarkably high average level in his songs. Indeed, perhaps he is best approached through them, for while his intuition is less acute, less immediate, than Schubert's, although he is less sensitive than Debussy or Mussorgsky, the energy of his imagination on these small canvases—which he liked best and which best suited him—is altogether outstanding.

With regard to this completeness, it should be said that the various linked pairs of Brahms *Lieder*, such as the two *Klänge* settings Op. 66 nos. 1 and 2, *Sommerabend* and *Mondenschein* Op. 85 nos. 1 and 2, or even the very early *Liebe und Frühling* Op. 3 nos. 2 and 3, ought always to be performed consecutively. It has been known for a singer to separate the two Op. 85 pieces by, of all things, *Auf dem Schiffe* Op. 97 no. 2, thus destroying the effect intended by Heine in his verses and Brahms with his music. As the composer said to Dessoff, 'Both poems come together in Heine's work [his *Heimkehr* of 1823–4]. The moon is a central figure in both, and it is annoying for a musician to have to use four good lines once only, when he might repeat them with suitable variations.' Other pairs that should not be separated are the duets *Weg der Liebe* Op. 20 nos. 1 and 2, the *Junge Lieder* songs Op. 63 nos. 5 and 6, the group of three called *Heimweh* Op. 63 nos. 7, 8 and 9, and the two songs with viola obbligato Op. 91. It is also best if *Regenlied* and *Nachklang* Op. 59 nos. 3 and 4 are performed together, for the latter begins with the same melody and then most expressively departs from it. (One need hardly add that the *Vier ernste Gesänge* Op. 121 ought not to be separated, or that the *Magelone Romanzen* Op. 33 produce their fullest effect when forming a recital by themselves.)

That Brahms's *Lieder* are all of a piece with the best aspects of the rest of his production will become more apparent when later we examine their separate elements, and this has already been suggested by the cross-references with his instrumental works already noted. Yet at the same time we find in them evidence of his purely personal interests of a sort he would not have allowed into his larger pieces; as instance of this is the quotation of four bars from a song by his friend Hermann Levi (who later became a great Wagner conductor) in *Dämmrung senkte sich von oben* Op. 59 no. 1. Note also the quotation from a

Scarlatti sonata in *Unüberwindlich* Op. 72 no. 5, a hint of Brahms's preoccupations with this composer: in an 1885 letter to Elisabet von Herzogenberg he said, 'I have over three hundred beautiful old manuscript copies [of Scarlatti's music], of which one hundred and seventy-two are unpublished', these originally being from the Abbate Santini's famous collection. We catch a glimpse, too, of Brahms the pianist and teacher in the Cramer *étude*-like figures of the accompaniment to *An die Tauben* Op. 63 no. 4, to *Blinde Kuh* Op. 58 no. 1, and also in *O komm, holde Sommernacht* Op. 58 no. 4. More private still are the references to *Regenlied* Op. 59 no. 3 and to *Wie Melodien zieht es* Op. 105 no. 1 in, respectively, the Violin Sonatas Nos. 1 and 2 Opp. 78 and 100; these, far from being (in Hanslick's words regarding Op. 78) the result of Brahms 'abandoning himself unconsciously to a reminiscence still active within him', were deliberately intended as affectionate tributes to his friend Klaus Groth, whose poetry both the songs use.

The *Lieder* also give us a better idea of Brahms's ideas on religion than do his larger works. Somewhat as the Ave Maria Op. 12 avoided setting the whole of the liturgical text, so the Requiem Op. 45 opposes Catholic ceremonial with its Dies Irae emphasis on the terrors of judgement day, substituting a memorial service whose main purpose is solace for the living. (In this respect it makes an interesting comparison with Delius's Requiem, using a text by Nietzsche, which flatly denies the possibility of another life.) In a footnote to his edition of Brahms's correspondence with Heinrich and Elisabet von Herzogenberg, Kalbeck tells us the composer always enjoyed 'seeking out godless texts in the Bible. Nothing made him angrier than to be taken for an orthodox church musician on account of his sacred works, and his *Vier ernste Gesänge* Op. 121 were not his only protest.' Brahms himself went further, and in connection with his search for texts said in a letter to Frau von Herzogenberg, 'They aren't heathenish enough for me in the Bible. I've bought the Koran, but can find nothing there either.' In the *Vier ernste Gesänge* (as in Schubert's *Die Winterreise* D. 911) there is an unflinching avoidance of emotional indulgence, yet in their rather distant attitude to the supposed consolations of religion these songs may be compared with the view implicit in Beethoven's oratorio *Christus im Oelberge* Op. 85. While making his position fairly clear in the Requiem Op. 45, Brahms is in every sense more uncompromising in his *Vier ernste Gesänge*, the last music he published and a work of deliberate farewell if ever there was one. Yet it is unlikely he would have gone so far in a large-scale piece. The only exception is the finale to his Symphony No. 4 Op. 98, where the tides of human suffering are submitted to the archaic formality of a passacaglia which is the more meaningful for coming after the phrygian modality of the slow movement with its hints of religion's alleged consolations. This finale's import, however, is stoical rather than religious; it is an expression not even of agnosticism but of abnegation—and the *Vier ernste Gesänge* tell us why, as earlier, and less clearly, had both the music and the texts chosen for his Motets Op. 74.

In his reconciliation of lyricism with the more formal—and form-building—elements of music, Brahms may have found some help in Beethoven, different though their gifts were. In songs like *Neue Liebe, neues Leben* Op. 75 no. 2 and *Mit einem gemalten Band* Op. 83 no. 3, Beethoven tried to adapt the sonata idea to the *Lied*'s emerging requirements. Fairly direct signs of this influence can be found in Brahms's *Agnes* Op. 59 no. 5, suggestive of Beethoven's *Busslied* Op. 48 no. 6, or Brahms's *In der Gasse* Op. 58 no. 6, with its opening distant echo of the Pastoral Symphony's third movement—*Lustiges Zusammensein der Landleute*. Probably more relevant to Brahms's purposes, though, were Schubert pieces like *Der Hirt auf dem Felsen* D. 965, a kind of vocal sonatina.

Lyricism is very much a question of melody and of line, however, and it was natural that Brahms should channel his melodic profusion into counterpoint. Instances have been cited of the unhappy results he occasionally obtained, yet often the effect was to give his lyricism a more powerful expression. Again, Schubert could provide a model—in pieces such as *Lied* D. 788, whose accompaniment begins in two-part counterpoint (duly followed up in Brahms's *Sommerfäden* Op. 72 no. 2)—as could Schumann, whose liking for canonic devices was almost a balance for the dream world so much of his finest music inhabits.

Often Brahms's counterpoint in vocal works arises out of the requirements of the text, as with the duet *Die Nonne und der*

Ritter Op. 28 no. 1, where each voice is treated as a distinct personality, with added effect when they are heard together. Or consider *Märznacht* Op. 44 no. 12, an SSAA setting of Uhland, in two sections, major and minor, each in canon and with one soprano and alto answered at three bars distance by the other; here the music, far from being dry, reflects the verses well, as in the chromatic phrases that portray the storm's raging. A similar case is *An die Heimat* Op. 64 no. 1, where a free canon is able to suggest the force with which the singer is drawn by the thought of home.

Quite often counterpoint arises from the need for rhythmic variety, an instance being the duet *Phänomen* Op. 61 no. 3, where there is canonic imitation in the central section; in another duet, *Klänge* Op. 66 no. 1, it produces a simpler sort of contrast—between the voices' counterpoint and the homophonic piano interludes. In the song *Mein wundes Herz verlangt nach milder Ruh* Op. 59 no. 7 considerable emotional intensity results from the keyboard's imitation of the voice, with diminution, augmentation and contrary motion. Sometimes one is reminded, if indirectly, of Robert Franz's careful complexity and preoccupation with unity—though he rarely achieved such unobtrusively natural-seeming effects as the double canon in Brahms's *Geistliches Lied* Op. 30 or the inversion of parts in *Letzes Glück* Op. 104 no. 4. Also worth mentioning are the smoothly flowing contrary motion between voices and piano in *Weg der Liebe* Op. 20 no. 2, the double counterpoint in (of all places) the keyboard Waltz Op. 39 no. 16, the graceful canonic lines of *Nachtwache* Op. 104 no. 2. A further example is the apparent spontaneity in employing learned devices in the Haydn Variations Op. 56, especially the fourth variation. All these are evidence, by the way, of skills which helped Brahms's Double Concerto Op. 102 avoid the diffuseness of Beethoven's Triple Concerto, Op. 56.

It is only an apparent paradox that in the happiest circumstances such techniques make the lyricism of Brahms's music all the more telling; furthermore it is an indication of the homogeneity of his finest work that the devices which help to emphasize this lyricism in his songs also go to shape his larger pieces. Proof of this, on a different level, are the very numerous cross-references between his instrumental works and *Lieder*; though a number of examples have already been given, others have particular relevance here. Such links, of course, are far from being unique to Brahms, and earlier and later instances can be found—the connection between the *Elegischer Gesang* Op. 118 and the slow movement to the 'Archduke' Trio Op. 97 of Beethoven, or between Schoenberg's song *Der Wanderer* Op. 6 no. 8 and his String Quartet No. 1 Op. 7. Comparable are Schubert's variations on his *Lied* called *Der Tod und das Mädchen* D. 531 in his String Quartet No. 14 D. 810, or the references to Janáček's opera *Katya Kabanova* in that composer's Violin Sonata. An illustration on a much larger scale is *Der fliegende Holländer*, which, according to Wagner, sprang from Senta's Ballad (itself considerably influenced by Loewe).

Regarding the way Brahms's Violin Sonata No. 1 Op. 78 appears to have grown somewhat comparably from the *Regenlied* Op. 59 no. 3, Billroth well said, 'The whole Sonata is to me like an echo of the song, like a fantasy about the song', and later, 'It is a piece of music entirely in elegy; the feeling and the motives are an echo of the *Regenlied*.' The last bars of *Es liebt sich so lieblich im Lenze* Op. 71 no. 1 also remind us of the violin sonata Op. 78's close; *Geheimnis*, No. 3 of that same group of songs, has a mood similar to that of the piano Capriccio Op. 76 no. 8, rather as the sombre colouring of *Verzagen* Op. 72 no. 4 anticipates that of the final keyboard works. Other songs which look forward to the Opp. 116–19 collections, particularly the gentle Intermezzo Op. 119 no. 1, are the last three items of Op. 106, *Es hing der Reif*, *Meine Lieder* and *Ein Wanderer*, and also *Mädchenlied* Op. 107 no. 5.

Similarly, the third movement of Brahms's Clarinet Trio Op. 114 looks back to the mood of his *Liebeslieder* Waltzes Opp. 52 and 65, in a way paralleled by the reminiscence of *Geliebter, wo zaudert dein irrender Fuss* Op. 33 no. 13 found most unexpectedly in the first movement of his stark Cello Sonata No. 1 Op. 38. There is also a hint of the *Liebeslieder* in his part-song *Wechsellied zum Tanze* Op. 31 no. 1. Again, in the Poco adagio of the Piano Quartet No. 2 Op. 26 we find an early instrumental example of the quintessentially Brahmsian lyrical intermezzo already prefigured in a few *Lieder* such as *An eine Äolsharfe* Op. 19 no. 5, and this is a good instance of the way his chamber music and songs afford parallel instances of his development more complete than those offered by any other categories of his output—even solo keyboard works. It is instructive, however, to contrast the two versions of *Der Gang zum Liebchen* (for solo singer Op. 48 no. 1 and for SATB Op. 31 no. 3) with the earlier Waltz Op. 39 no. 5 for piano, of whose music they are an amplification, and also the *Lied*, Op. 48 no. 6, and part-song, Op. 62 no. 7, versions of *Vergangen ist mir Glück und Heil*.

These points may be confirmed, on a different level, by comparing Brahms's very characteristic use of the diminished seventh in this same Poco adagio (of Op. 26) with its use in *Lieder* such as *Frühlingstrost* Op. 63 no. 1 or in the Intermezzo Op. 118 no. 6. These particular procedures, it might be added, almost certainly come from Schubert's use of diminished sevenths, augmented sixths and other chords in non-functional ways for atmospheric purposes, as in the keyboard prelude to *Am Meer* D. 957. This, incidentally, is a song that is echoed in the E major theme of the slow movement to the original version of Brahms's Piano Trio No. 1 Op. 8.

Considerably more devious links can be discovered between works from quite different periods of Brahms's life. For example, with simple octave transpositions the first theme of his Symphony No. 4 Op. 98 may be shown as deriving from the same basic idea as the Andante espressivo of his Piano Sonata No. 3 Op. 5:

In somewhat the same way, the descent of the vocal line at the words 'hell, so hell' in *Ade!* Op. 85 no. 4 recalls a similar passage in *Der Überläufer* Op. 48 no. 2 at 'wollen wir gehen'. Less specifically, the powerful *Auf dem Kirchhofe* Op. 105 no. 4 anticipates the *Vier ernste Gesänge* Op. 121 while at the same time glancing back to the Violin Sonata No. 2 Op. 100 and beyond that to the piano Capriccio Op. 76 no. 1. Perhaps because of their very amplitude, links can be discovered between several of the *Magelone Romanzen* Op. 33 and *Lieder* from later phases of Brahms's output; for example, between

So willst du des Armen dich gnädig erbarmen Op. 33 no. 5 and *Feldeinsamkeit* Op. 86 no. 2, between *War es dir, dem diese Lippen bebten* Op. 33 no. 7—especially the passage at 'alle Sinne nach den Lippen strebten'—and the Daumer settings of Op. 57, or between *Ruhe, Süssliebchen* Op. 33 no. 9 and *Geistliches Wiegenlied* Op. 91 no. 2.

In several other pairs of songs it is also possible to find the composer using the same idea or process in different ways. For example, almost at the close of *Heimkehr* Op. 7 no. 6, at the sudden shift to the major, and in the *Weg der Liebe* duet Op. 20 no. 1 at the words 'Kommt Liebe, sie wird siegen/Und finden den Weg'. Or in *Vorüber* Op. 58 no. 7 at 'in den süsseste Traum' and in *Mädchenlied* Op. 107 no. 5 at 'Die Tränen rinnen mir übers Gesicht' near the end. There are also definite melodic resemblances between *Phänomen* Op. 61 no. 3, at 'farbig beschattet' and 'doch wirst du lieben' and the *Minnelied* Op. 71 no. 5, and, improbable as it may seem, between the accompaniments of *Der Schmied* Op. 19 no. 4 and of *Salome* Op. 69 no. 8. Finally, there is a very obvious link between Brahms's *Von ewiger Liebe* Op. 43 no. 1 and an unpublished wedding chorus he had written some ten years earlier in Hamburg—an indication of his willingness to return to and re-work old material. Relevant sections of the two melody lines are given here:

Brahms 1858

Das Haus be-ne -dei' ich und preis' es laut, das emp-

fan-gen hat ei-ne lieb -li-che Braut

Brahms Op. 43 no. 1 (circa 1868)

Ei-sen und Stahl,— man schmiedet sie um,

.un-se-re Lie-be, wer wan-delt sie um?

Brahms's melodies often show a less acute sensitivity than those of his contemporaries such as Berlioz, Liszt or Mussorgsky, and whereas those of, say, Bruckner or Schubert (to name composers within his own tradition), are normally long and supple, his often prove to be made up of short asymmetrical components. Bruckner's melodies can be broken down, too, but usually his winding, soaring lines dissolve arpeggios into stepwise movement on a vast scale while with Brahms the arpeggio figures remain, and divide the melodies into harmonic segments which, as it were, stay rooted to the ground. At the same time, the structure and direction of his melodic shapes is nearly always clear, even when they are interrupted for breathing, as in the songs or clarinet music, or when they are broken with rests, as in *Juchhe!* Op. 6 no. 4, *Nicht mehr zu dir zu gehen, beschloss ich* Op. 32 no. 2, or in the last movement of his Violin Sonata No. 3 Op. 108.

When his melodies are sustained, as in the reflective passages of such works as the Piano Trio No. 1 Op. 8 (original version), the String Sextet No. 1 Op. 18 or even his Cello Sonata No. 1 Op. 38 (which should be compared in general style with the opening melodies of Beethoven's Piano Trio No. 6 'Archduke' or Schubert's Piano Sonata No. 21 D. 960), this usually signals that the work is to be on an extensive time-scale, but even in a contemplative setting the triadic leaps convey strength and energy. Generally, however, Brahms's melodies only learnt to flow easily with time, as he became more concise—an interesting, though only apparent, contradiction. In fact, while he often restricted his melodic material in its basic form, he was constantly able to draw new shapes from it which contributed to the effect of the whole—whether the work happened to be a large or a small one. Thus the descending and ascending thirds which make up the opening theme of his Symphony No. 4 Op. 98 (see Ex. p. 77) also play a considerable part in the shaping of the entire movement, and for such economy to work material has to be readily transformable. The familiar case of Beethoven's Symphony No. 5 Op. 67 shows how a brief motive can imprint itself on the memory so that its variants and derivatives can easily be recognized. Brahms also had precedents in Schubert *Lieder* such as *Memnon* D. 541, where most of the accompaniment evolves from the opening prelude, or in *Der zürnenden Diana* D. 707, from the very first bar. The mutability of motives allows everything in a musical fabric to be essential. This is especially the case within a contrapuntal situation of the sort often favoured by Brahms as, say the melodic and rhythmic alterations undergone by the counter-subject of Beethoven's *Grosse Fuge* Op. 133 show; a relevant later instance is the *Litanei* movement of Schoenberg's String Quartet No. 2 Op. 10, where extraordinary variations of the basic material are accomplished.

Particularly in his songs, however, Brahms does sometimes make an interesting use of static—that is unchanged—motives, although these too are normally of great simplicity. An example is the fifth—F sharp to B—always differently harmonized, in *Mit vierzig Jahren* Op. 94 no. 1. Another case of a predominating interval is the sixth—A to F sharp (and vice versa)—in *Frühlingstrost* Op. 63 no. 1, and we should also note the recurring motive in the last song of this same opus, *Ich sah als Knabe Blumen blühn*—taken, perhaps unconsciously, from Schubert's *Die Taubenpost* D. 957. Further instances are the ascending figure in *Klage* Op. 69 no. 2 and the repeated basses, very rare with Brahms, of *Über die Heide* Op. 86 no. 4 and *Es hing der Reif* Op. 106 no. 3.

But as we might expect from the composer's variational powers, exact repetition is rare in this music. Twelve whole bars are repeated in *War es dir, dem diese Lippen bebten* Op. 33 no. 7 at the words 'Blick und Lächeln schwangen Flügel', and in *O wüsst' ich doch den Weg zurück* Op. 63 no. 8 there is repetition at three points, yet thematic economy is normally the rule. An obvious example is the pair of songs *Scheiden und Meiden* and *In der Ferne* Op. 19 nos. 2 and 3, which are based on the same material, while in the piano Intermezzo Op. 118 no. 6 Brahms achieves an almost symphonic breadth, despite the work's brevity. As with Chopin earlier and Webern later, this is a case, as are his finest *Lieder*, of large music on a small scale; this is made possible by the adaptability of the main theme, which is varied in many ways yet without losing its character. (This Intermezzo should be compared with the Adagio mesto, in the same key, of the Horn Trio Op. 40.) Other instances of thematic economy are *Regenlied* Op. 59 no. 3 or *Über die Heide* Op. 86 no. 4, where, in combination with the repeated bass mentioned above, it produces a striking impression of con-trolled energy.

Such effects are not easily obtained, for as Brahms said to the young Richard Strauss, 'To construct a melodic shape is a matter of talent, but here we are also concerned with one of the most difficult technical problems . . . a melody which seems to have been born in a moment is nearly always the result of intensive labour.' Strauss himself echoed this closely a good many years later: 'Two bars of music come to me spontaneously, then I continue spinning this thread, placing brick upon brick . . . this sometimes takes a very long while. A melody that seems born in a moment is almost invariably the result of hard work.' Certainly this is confirmed, on close examination, by such apparently self-generating melodies of Brahms as *Meine Lieder* Op. 106 no. 4, by the second theme of the opening *Allegro* of his Piano Quartet No. 3 Op. 60, whose forty bars' length is made up of an eight-bar idea with four variants, or by the second theme of the first movement to his Symphony No. 3 Op. 90, which has seven variants on a one-bar motive. In German vocal music this tradition goes back perhaps to the thematic continuity of some of Haydn's canzonets, and it is instructive to contrast the repetitions of *Mädchenlied* Op. 85 no. 3 with the unobtrusive melodic development of *Am Sonntag Morgen* Op. 49 no. 1, another melody with interruptions, and, more impressive, of *Mein wundes Herz verlangt nach milder Ruh* Op. 59 no. 7. The effect is particularly striking in a *Lied* such as *Botschaft* Op. 47 no. 1, where the extension of the melody near the close adds a new dimension to the song— even if this is not a particularly good setting of the poem (Hafiz translated by Daumer) as such. An earlier instance is *Treue Liebe* Op. 7 no. 1, where there is a fresh and well managed elaboration in the final verse.

It must be admitted, however, that this kind of linear writing often leads to melodies of a decidedly instrumental, rather than vocal, character. Though he did not emulate pieces such as Mendelssohn's *Die erste Walpurgisnacht* Op. 60 (itself modelled on the dramatic cantatas of Andreas Romberg), Brahms's choral works are as rewarding to sing as those of Mendelssohn or Handel, especially when, like the exquisite part-songs of his Op. 104, they are on a small scale. But this often is not so with his solo songs. True, the sound of a contralto voice may seem as inseparable from the melody of his *Sapphische Ode* Op. 94 no. 4 as the oboe's tone does from the slow movement of his Violin Concerto Op. 77, yet the widely arching, instrumental melody, however beautiful in itself, is scarcely appropriate to the tender sentiments of Hans Schmidt's verses and calls for instrumental powers of sostenuto.

In connection with the melody at 'Was lispeln die Winde' in *Gestillte Sehnsucht* Op. 91 no. 1, Elisabet von Herzogenberg wrote to Brahms that this 'is very difficult even for a talented singer. Why are you so cruel, turning women into oboes or violins? Is this why you begin with B like that other cruel man [Beethoven]? How gratefully the throat relaxes at *"Sie lispeln die Welt in Schlummer"*.' Billroth nicely put it the other way round when speaking of the Violin Sonata No. 1 Op. 78, saying, 'What a voice for the violin!' *Auf dem See* Op. 106 no. 2 actually sounds better on the violin, as Frau von Herzogenberg discovered. But she might equally have complained of some other nineteenth-century composers for such instrumental melodies have a parallel in the operas of Dvořák and Smetana, whose vocal lines sometimes appear to have been conceived without regard to the singers or the words. This is also true of composers more immediately associated with writing for the voice, and we find awkward drops of a seventh and a ninth, for example, in Cinna's aria from Act I of Spontini's *La Vestale*. We should also note the instrumental, almost scherzo-like character of part of the melody of Schubert's *Das Heimweh* D. 851. Brahmsian phrases like these

Brahms Op. 53

Brahms Op. 121 no. 4

have a more immediate precedent in such Schubert *Lieder* as *Wasserflut* or *Der greise Kopf*, both from *Die Winterreise* D. 911.

In the latter song, for example, Müller's image of the snow making the lover suddenly white-haired is suggested by a leap of a thirteenth on the piano, an eleventh in the voice.

There is no objection to the horn effects at '*Ruh'n sie?*' and '*Sie ruh'n*' in *Nachtwache* Op. 104 no. 2, and the four notes at the beginning of *Klänge* Op. 66 no. 2 which are identical with the start both of the Andante and the Scherzo of Brahms's Piano Sonata No. 2 Op. 2 are merely coincidental, but a number of his other song melodies are rather too noticeably instrumental in contour.

Varied examples are the *Lied aus dem Gedicht 'Ivan'* Op. 3 no. 4, *Des Liebsten Schwur* Op. 69 no. 4, and *Frühlingslied* Op. 85 no. 5. In the case of *Wie soll ich die Freude, die Wonne denn tragen*, Op. 33 no. 6, an instrumental-styled melody appropriately gives rise to an accompaniment which almost asks to be orchestrated, while that of *Dein blaues Auge hält so still* Op. 59 no. 8 suggests string rather than vocal writing. In a number of instances melody and accompaniment seem, partly because of this sort of melodic construction, to be rather independent of each other. With *Sommerfäden* Op. 72 no. 2, for example, the singer's melody sounds like something imposed on the two-part invention of the accompaniment, rather as, on a much larger scale, in many passages of Wagner's operas the voice seems an inessential addition to a work unfolding chiefly in orchestral terms. Certainly the accompaniment is the real musical basis of *An ein Bild* Op. 63 no. 3, and the melody means little by itself in comparison with, say, that of *Junge Lieder*, No. 6 of the same group. Similarly, while the total effect of *Feldeinsamkeit* Op. 86 no. 2 is very beautiful, it is hard to ignore the fact that the vocal melody, especially in the middle section, has little life of its own. Occasionally, however, this effect is good, as in *Agnes* Op. 59 no. 5, where the composer's whole approach to Mörike's poem is such that the accompaniment must tell us much that the melody does not; *Anklänge* Op. 7 no. 3 is a much earlier and slightly better instance.

In many cases, although Brahms's melodies are harmonically conceived, the actual harmonization has singular independence. Non-harmonic notes such as free appoggiaturas are not at once resolved, and leaps such as his characteristic sixths intensify the melody's independent expression. At the same time, he liked harmonic substitutions that replaced chords with others of comparable tonal effect but which eventually, when the piece was on a large enough scale, changed the entire harmonization of the melody. Yet sometimes, with a glance forward to serial technique, he retains the melodic intervals and changes all the other elements—of harmony, rhythm, and so on. As an example of close argument consider the part-song *Und gehst du über den Kirchhof* Op. 44 no. 10, where the whole of the minor section derives from the motive with which the altos enter, the—admittedly ad lib—accompaniment taking the form of a simple note-series. (For emphatically Brahmsian contrast, the major-keyed section has a plain harmonization as support.)

A different kind of organization, though equally strict in its way, is found in *Unbewegte laue Luft* Op. 57 no. 8. This is in two parts that might at first seem unrelated, yet the passionate second portion is actually based on material suitably transformed from the dreamy opening. Notice also how the melody of the middle section of *Ruhe, Süssliebchen* Op. 33 no. 9, at 'Murmelt fort, ihr Melodien' derives from the opening motive, how the whole of the Magelone cycle is drawn together by the reference in the final *Treue Liebe dauert lange* (No. 15) to the opening *Keinen hat es noch gereut*, and how extra cohesion is given to *Von ewiger Liebe* Op. 43 no. 1 by the voice echoing and developing the keyboard's phrases.

Many further instances could be given of the closely-knit organization of these *Lieder*. For example, in *Wie rafft' ich mich auf in der Nacht* Op. 32 no. 1 at the words 'Der Mühlbach rauschte durch felsigen Schacht' there is a meaningful return by the piano bass to the voice's opening phrase. Further examples are *Regenlied* and *Nachklang* Op. 59 nos. 3 and 4, both of which grow from very brief keyboard figures. A different case is *Eine gute, gute Nacht* Op. 59 no. 6, the two verses of which are differently set but with a hint of the opening theme in the penultimate line of the second; this is slightly reminiscent of Schubert's *Fischerweise* D. 881, which sets its verses alternately with two different melodies, each varied. Both songs should perhaps be regarded as derivatives, or rather developments, of strophic form.

The relations between melody and harmony, and between thematic material and structural process, give rise to the question of folk song and its rôle in nineteenth-century art music. This is obviously a matter of particular interest where the *Lied* is concerned, though, as we have seen, German musical traditions were nearly always resistant to outside influences, even when from as close to home as this. Social, political and literary currents at this time led to a new concern with folk art and beside these nationalism was an attempt to render music more acutely expressive through the use of local, regional traits. As such, it was like other aspects of Romanticism, a move against the eighteenth century and the belief that its international, seemingly universal, language was one of music's prime characteristics; this was expressed, for instance, by Gluck when he said he wanted to eliminate the 'ridiculous difference' that existed between the various national musics, and by Haydn when he said 'My language is understood all over the world.'

As usual, Brahms's attitude was ambivalent, because what attracted him was not the heightened expressiveness—the established resources of art music and the developments leading directly from them were quite enough for him—but folk music's (or what he believed to be folk music's) echoes of past melodic innocence. With that lack of interest in the music of other countries which is typical of German composers, Brahms was scarcely aware that abroad the movement was essentially one of liberation from the dominance of German technical methods. Nor was he conscious of the fact that in, say, Russia, composers were experiencing considerable difficulties either in devising new structural procedures or in adapting existing (German) ones to folk material. Despite this, Brahms's *Lieder* show that even German composers themselves encountered the latter problem, which in his particular case was compounded, as we shall see, by a confusion as to what did or did not constitute the folk music of his native country.

A number of his songs, like *Volkslieder* and *Die Trauernde* Op. 7 nos. 4 and 5, are in dialect, but Brahms was not the first German composer to set what were then believed to be folk poems. Weber had used eleven texts from the (considerably re-written and re-worked) *Knaben Wunderhorn* collection of Arnim and Brentano, and Robert Burns had inspired Schumann's best folk song settings (Opp. 25 and 27). Brahms appeared to be rather strict when dealing with folk poems, for although with verses of more sophisticated origin he made, as

85

we shall see, frequent and sometimes quite arbitrary changes, when setting *Guter Rat* as his Op. 75 no. 2 he restored a number of passages Brentano and Arnim had altered or omitted. In fact, this was rather pointless, for it has been shown that a great many so-called folk poems, even before undergoing modification by such collectors, were corrupted art poems that had become common property—and this was especially the case in Germany.

By contrast, this preoccupation with authenticity, however misplaced, did not trouble Brahms where music was concerned, least of all in the collections of folk songs he published under his own name (though without opus number). As with Liszt in his *Magyar Dallok* and Hungarian Rhapsodies, Brahms's attitude, like that of Weber in his operas, was that of a creative musician, not that of a scholar, and it was only in a later generation that men such as Bartók and Kodály were able to combine both rôles. Thus *Dornröschen*, the very first of his *Volkskinderlieder*, is a fake by Zuccalmaglio (of whom more later), as is also *Dem Schutzengel*, the last item in this set. Similarly *Heidenröslein* and *Das Mädchen und die Hasel* from this same collection, far from being folk songs, are the work of Reichardt, a composer of the *Zweite Berliner Liederschule*.

Misunderstandings about the authenticity of folk material were fairly widespread among nineteenth-century musicians, particularly in Germany, and are partly explained by the many faulty editions, often of high repute, that were in circulation. The themes usually cited as illustrations of the influence of folk song on Brahms, such as the rondo melody of his String Sextet No. 1 Op. 18, the opening theme of his String Quintet No. 1 Op. 88, or *Ständchen* Op. 106 no. 1, are nothing of the sort, and simply resemble what he and many others thought was folk music. In fact, these and many other cases have rather more sophisticated models, the Sextet melody's ancestor, for example, being the rondo theme of Schubert's Piano Trio No. 1 D. 898, which is even in the same key. Similarly, the parent of the Andante theme of his Piano Quintet Op. 34 is Schubert's *Pause* from *Die schöne Müllerin* D. 795, while that of the finale to his Symphony No. 2 Op. 73 is the last movement of Haydn's Symphony No. 104. There are resemblances between the D minor Vivace sections of the second movement

to his Violin Sonata No. 2 Op. 100 (1886) and Grieg's Violin
Sonata No. 1 Op. 8 (1865). Sometimes the origin of Brahms's
inventions lies in Brahms himself, as may be seen by comparing
the first subject of his Symphony No. 2 with that of the Violin
Concerto Op. 77; see also the long series of trills for the soloist
in the latter and that in his Piano Concerto No. 2 Op. 83.
(Other examples of the many cross-references between
Brahms's works have already been given.)

Despite false scents in the music of Brahms and other German composers, nationalism in music became a force elsewhere
earlier than is generally recognized, as the distinctly Russian
traits in the church music of Bortniansky (1751–1825) suggest.
The use of regional, or supposedly regional, traits was also
extremely widespread, as the echoes of Amazonian–Indian
melodies in *Il Guaraný* by Gomes or Gottschalk's pianistic
reflections of the culture of the Caribbean and American
Gulf Coast show. Under these circumstances it would have
been remarkable if even Brahms had been wholly unaffected,
but not too much should be made of national characteristics in
folk as distinct from art music. Similarities of melodic and
rhythmic vocabulary have been shown between Brazilian and
Russian tunes, between Arabian and Scots folk melodies,
between music from Anatolia and from Hungary.

Yet the use of such music should not be dismissed as mere
'antique-fancying', for however mishandled by German composers, the modality of folk song had a significant rôle in such
works as Chopin's mazurkas, and in many pieces by nationalist
writers like Mussorgsky. An idea of how much folk music
contributed to Bartók's art can be gained by comparing the
incongruity between the essentially monodic folk melodies and
the Straussian chromaticism of his Suite No. 2 Op. 4 with the
perfect integration of his mature works. In contrast, the
modality of the Scots, Irish, Russian, Spanish, Italian and
Portuguese folk tunes set by Beethoven is quite indifferently
violated by his diatonic harmonizations, and even the *Heiliger
Dankgesang eines Genesenen an die Gottheit in der lydischen Tonart*
of his String Quartet No. 15 Op. 132 led nowhere. Brahms's
Ach, arme Welt Op. 110 no. 2, with its D natural in F minor
giving a dorian flavour, shows, like his phrygian theme in the
Symphony No. 4 Op. 98, a greater sensitivity than Beethoven's
and many similar folk melody settings; however, a case like

87

Klosterfräulein Op. 61 no. 2 which demands but does not get a phrygian cadence is more typical.

As the sophistications of supposed folk elements in his Op. 14 *Lieder* suggest, when Brahms set a poem of folk or popular character the result only rarely gave rise to the simplicity of melodic phraseology that we find in, say, Mahler's Symphony No. 4. Even when the melody is quite folkish, as in *Der Schmied* Op. 19 no. 4 or *Sonntag* Op. 47 no. 3, with its three sixteen-bar verses all consisting of four lines of four bars each, it receives a consciously artistic *Lieder* accompaniment. A specific example is *In stiller Nacht*, No. 42 of his *49* (so-called) *Deutsche Volkslieder*, which as well as being largely composed by Brahms himself (on the basis of a religious melody that appeared in several collections published during his lifetime) has again a highly *Lieder*-orientated, unfolklike accompaniment. Simplicity of melody and rhythm is a prime quality of actual German folk music, echoing Luther's hymns with their characteristically Protestant reduction of the subtleties of Gregorian chant and the simple metres of German medieval poetry (compared with that of other countries); but these have little real place amid the complexities of Brahms. When they do tend to simplicity, his themes are usually *Ländler*- or waltz-like, there being three such instances in the first movement of his String Sextet No. 1 Op. 18. Certainly it is quite hard to find in his compositions the innocent melodies which recur in Schubert and Mahler and which represent important facets of their musical personalities. Still less, despite that quotation from Gung'l, already noted, in *Minnelied* Op. 71 no. 5 or the echo of a popular song by Baumann in the *Wiegenlied* Op. 49 no. 4, is there anything like Mahler's nostalgic evocations of street and café music. Of interest here is a comparison between a genuinely old German melody—published during 1542 at Nuremberg in Berg and Newber's *68 Lieder*—and Brahms's setting of the same words for two voices:

Anon.

Ich weiss mir ein Maid-lein hübsch und fein. Hüt' du dich!___ Ich weiss mir ein

Maid-lein hübsch und fein, es kann wohl falsch und freundlich sein. Hüt' du dich!

Lebhaft, heimlich und schalkhaft — Brahms Op.66 no.5

'Ich weiss ein Mäd-lein hübsch.. und fein... hüt du dich! hüt du dich! Ich weiss ein Mäd-lein hübsch.. und fein,... es kann wohl falsch und freund - lich__ sein, hüt du dich! hüt du dich__ ver-(ver-) trau 'ihr nicht,__ sie nar - ret dich.

Similarly, *Da unten im Tale*, No. 6 of the *49 Deutsche Volkslieder* and one of the few genuine folk melodies in that collection, should be set beside *Trennung* Op. 97 no. 6, Brahms's setting of the same words. No. 31, *Dort in den Weiden steht ein Haus*, is almost certainly a forgery by Zuccalmaglio, and may be compared with Brahms's Op. 97 no. 4, his own setting of the text, which bears the same title. Other cases where these so-called folk songs may be contrasted with Brahms's independent settings are *Maria ging aus Wandern*, No. 14, whose melody almost certainly is by Zuccalmaglio but which has a genuinely old text, set for mixed choir as *Marias Wallfahrt* Op. 22 no. 3, and No. 4, *Guten Abend*, quite certainly a Zuccalmaglio forgery, whose words are also used for *Spannung* Op. 84 no. 5. In most cases the songs of his earlier solo collection, the *Volkskinderlieder*, are furnished with aptly simple accompaniments, in contrast with, say, *Erlaube mir, fein's Mädchen* or *Gunhilde*, Nos. 2 and 7 of the *49 Deutsche Volkslieder*, which again are too consciously artistic.

The sources of the *Volkskinderlieder* are two volumes of *Deutsche Volkslieder mit ihren Original-Weisen* published in Berlin during 1840 which, although full of arbitrary alterations by the editors, were highly regarded by Brahms and others. For example, besides faithfully reproducing a number of misprints in the texts, he even retained Zuccalmaglio's unsuitably high key for No. 11, *Wiegenlied*, despite its appearing at more apt pitch in the superior and earlier collections of Tchiska and Schottky (*Osterreichische Volkslieder*, 1818) or Erk and Irmer

(*Deutsche Volkslieder*, 1838). All these versions of the *Wiegenlied*, rather than being of folk origin, however, derive from Reichardt's *Schlaf, Kindchen, schlaf.* Several other *Volkskinderlieder* are not particularly old by the standards of folk music, an instance being *Sandmännchen*, No. 4, which is based on a melody from the *Geistlicher Psalter* published at Strasbourg in 1697. The music of others, such as *Dornröschen* and *Marienwürmchen*, Nos. 1 and 13, was forged by Zuccalmaglio, while in cases like *Weihnachten* and *Dem Schutzengel*, Nos. 12 and 14, both melody and text are his.

Two other points should be made here. Firstly, both true and false German folk music are united by a strain of sentimentality which may be traced back to the *Locheimer Liederbuch* collection of circa 1450. And secondly, Brahms's concern with such melodies can be related to the patriotism which grew on him as he became older. He developed a great admiration for Bismarck, and even for Blücher and Moltke, and eventually became Honorary President of the Viennese branch of the *Zum Ausspannen der Pferde*, a kind of Bismarck fan club, and rarely travelled without a volume of Bismarck's letters or speeches. It has to be remembered that he grew up during a time of increasing tension between Austria and Prussia within the loosely-knit German Confederation, and as a native of the free Hanseatic city of Hamburg, had no particular sympathy with the Prussian view; when open conflict occurred in 1866 he was equally critical of both sides. But the patriotic fervour accompanying the entirely unjust attack on France in 1870 engulfed Brahms, as it did virtually all Germans, and he later said to Henschel that 'After our first great defeat [at Saarbrücken] I was determined to join the army as a volunteer.' The patriotic aspect of his *Fest- und Gedenksprüche* Op. 109 is rather crude, but the Op. 55 *Triumphlied* is easily the most objectionable of Brahms's works in this category.

The influence upon it of Handel's Dettingen Te Deum, composed in 1743 to celebrate another victory over the French (by the English), has already been mentioned, and it is interesting to reflect that in writing the *Triumphlied*, one of his very few pieces inspired by an external, non-musical event, Brahms may have chosen his model quite deliberately. However, where Handel used an English text rather than the liturgical Latin, Brahms sought, despite his own lack of faith, to lend religious justification to France's brutal defeat by selecting his text from the Bible—principally the nineteenth chapter of Revelations, which celebrates the triumph over Babylon. He was persuaded by friends to omit the more extreme of the Evangelist's exultations over the hated city's downfall, but he wrote them into his own copy of the score and drew attention to them whenever possible. This well accords with the gradual coarsening of Brahms's outward manner referred to earlier, but his *Triumphlied* remains the only direct expression of it, his work otherwise maintaining its usual duality almost to the end.

The *Volkskinderlieder* were published in 1858, the *49 Deutsche Volkslieder* much later, in 1894. This latter was among the few of his productions that Brahms would ever admit to liking—though his good opinion of *Vergebliches Ständchen* Op. 84 no. 4 suggests that he was no more objective about his work than anyone else. The oldest of the three collections he drew upon for the *49 Volkslieder* was published by one Nicolai in 1777–8. Nicolai strongly disapproved of the concern with folk song which was already becoming apparent, and as an adverse criticism of the movement brought out his collection under the satirical title of *Eyn feyner kleyner Almanach Vol schönerr echterr liblicherr Volcklieder*, all the melodies being parodies composed either by Reichardt or himself. Many of these tunes, now with regional places of origin falsely ascribed, were later incorporated into the other two collections Brahms used, published by Zuccalmaglio and Kretzschmer, and so passed into his own *49 Deutsche Volkslieder*.

Thus we have the spectacle of a great composer lending his name to the folk status of material originally produced as a satire on folk music. In addition to the already-mentioned *Da unten im Tale* (No. 6) the only genuine specimens among Brahms's *49 Deutsche Volkslieder* are *Schönster Schatz, mein Engel* (20), *Mir ist ein schöns brauns Maidelein* (24), *All mein Gedanken* (30), which appears in the *Locheimer Liederbuch*, *Es steht ein Lind* (41) and probably *Ach, englische Schäferin* (8) and *Schöner Augen schöne Strahlen* (39). By including several of these Brahms contradicted his adverse comments on earlier collections such as those of Büsching and Hagen, or Erk, for Nos. 8 and 39 appear in the former, Nos. 6 and 20 in the latter. Yet besides accepting the parodies and various other kinds of forgery that occur in the Kretzschmer and Zuccalmaglio collections, in his correspondence Brahms attacked the uncorrupted material brought out by scholars such as Silcher (1826), Ditfurth (1855), besides Hagen and Büsching (1807) and particularly Erk (*Deutscher Liederhort*, 1856) and Böhme (*Altdeutsches Liederbuch*, 1877). Of these last two he wrote to Bächtold, 'They have long set the tone, and a very philistine one it is . . . my collection is definitely in opposition to them'. Later the weight of evidence forced Brahms to admit that possibly some of Zuccalmaglio's material was not genuine, yet he did not seem unduly concerned. Thus referring to *Wach auf, mein Hort*, which figures as No. 13 of the *49 Deutsche Volkslieder* despite being concocted by Reichardt for Nicolai's satirical venture, Brahms wrote to Spitta, 'Not really folk music? Well then, we have one good composer the more.'

Actually not one, but several composers: *Sagt mir, o schönste Schäfrin mein* (No. 1), *Gar lieblich hat sich gesellet* (3), *Jungfräulein, soll ich mit euch gehn* (11), *Wach auf, mein Hort* (13), *Wach auf, mein Herzensschöne* (16), *So wünsch ich ihr ein gute Nacht* (18), *Nur ein Gesicht auf Erden lebt* (19), *So will ich frisch und fröhlich sein* (32) and *Ich weiss mir 'n Maidlein* (40) were all composed by Reichardt for Nicolai's *feyner kleyner Almanach. Es ging ein Maidlein zarte* (21) and *Es reit ein Herr und auch sein Knecht* (28) are by Nicolai himself, while *Es ritt ein Ritter* (10), though of uncertain authorship, is also from that same satirical book. Among the rest, *Guten Abend* (4), *Feinsliebchen, du sollst mir nicht barfuss gehn* (12), *Schwesterlein* (15), *Es wohnet ein Fiedler* (36), *Des Abends kann ich nicht schlafen gehn* (38), *Es stunden drei Rosen* (43), *Es ging sich unsre Fraue, Nachtigall, sag* and *Verstohlen geht der Mond auf* (47–9) were all manufactured by Zuccalmaglio for his collections, *Maria ging aus Wandern* (14), *Wo gehst du hin, du Stolze?* (22), *Mein Mädel hat einen Rosenmund* (25), *Dort in den Weiden steht ein Haus* (31), *Dem Himmel will ich klagen, Es sass ein schneeweiss Vögelein* and *Es war einmal ein Zimmergesell* (44–6) probably are his. *Ach Gott, wie weh tut Scheiden* (17) is a similar case, having been composed by Groos and included in the *Deutsche Lieder für Jung und Alt* (Berlin, 1819) which he edited with Stein; *Du mein einzig Licht* (37) was written by Heinrich Albert in 1648, and *Die Sonne scheint nicht mehr* (5) is a conflation of several pieces.

The truth is that the pre-artistic rigidity of authentic material carefully preserved by real scholars could not meaningfully be related to the dialectical subtleties of modern German compositional technique—least of all as it was represented by Brahms. This was one occasion on which he could not reconcile the opposites. Even Chopin, who had a far greater understanding of his native folk music than Brahms, and much of whose output is permeated with its spirit (and whose artistic aims were very different from those of any German composer) only once quoted an actual folk melody in one of his pieces, and that was a youthful, posthumously-published work (the Mazurka Op. 68 no. 3).

When Brahms said, as he did repeatedly, that when he wished to invent a theme he called to mind the melodies of German folk music he was deceiving himself. What he really summoned up was corrupted or forged material which accorded with the sophistications of the German art music tradition. As his comments on Böhme, Erk and others make clear, real folk melodies would not have suited him at all. To say this is not adversely to criticize his compositions, but only to recognize that so completely do they embody the principles of their own tradition as to leave room for nothing else. Obviously, this is a source both of strength and weakness.

Thus Brahms's use of so-called Hungarian idioms was virtually certain to be unconvincing, even though he resorted to them almost throughout his career. Although earlier instances of its use in serious composition may be found, such as the finale to Hummel's Piano Sonata Op. 81—where it accords badly with the Bachian fugal elements of the second subject—Brahms was probably introduced to the style by the violinist Reményi during their 1853 tour. Its widespread use by Raff, Brahms and many others was really a kind of exotic seasoning, like the supposedly 'Turkish' music by Mozart and Beethoven, the 'Persian' music of Glinka's *Russlan and Ludmilla* or the exploitation of 'Spanish' rhythms and melodies by French composers. As later research by Kodály, Bartók and others showed, this was not Hungarian at all but a combination of *verbunkos*, Gypsy and (genuine) Turkish elements. *Verbunkos*, far from having folk origins, arose about the middle of the eighteenth century in the music played by the Gypsy string ensembles that accompanied Austrian army recruiting officers

from one Hungarian village to another. It was later popular-
ized by Gypsy orchestras in larger towns and was taken up
first by light composers and then for more serious music.

In this connection Brahms's *Zigeunerlieder* Op. 103 (in either
the SATB or solo voice and piano versions) further illustrate
how ill-focused his interest in folk music of any sort was. This
work might, in some ways, be considered more Bohemian than
Hungarian. The texts are taken from an undated Budapest
publication, *25 Ungarische Volkslieder für mittlere Stimme, Die
Klavier-Begleitung von Zoltán Nagy*, and comparison between this
and Op. 103 shows few Hungarian (Gypsy) characteristics
survived in Brahms's melodies. What we do find are firstly
irregular groupings of three, five and seven bars, secondly
much syncopation, and thirdly unconvincing imitations of the
cymbalom;* these first two characteristics, of course, appear
very frequently elsewhere in his music. Brahms's Hungarian
Dances for piano (to which, like his folk song collections, he
significantly gave no opus numbers) and his response to the
Op. 103 texts suggest, as do Couperin's Italian-styled dance
movements, that there are certain temperamental barriers
which cannot be crossed, and the sensibility these works express
remains just what we should expect from the most Teutonic
of composers.

A similar comment applies to the supposedly 'Hungarian'
qualities of *Der Frühling* Op. 6 no. 2, *Magyarisch* Op. 46 no. 2
or *Die Schwestern* Op. 61 no. 1, as it does to the 'Slavonic'
elements some commentators have managed to discover in
Klage Op. 69 no. 1, *Mädchenfluch* Op. 69 no. 9 or *Vorschneller
Schwur* Op. 95 no. 5. But needless to say, throughout the
entire Brahms literature his 'Hungarian' works are extrava-
gantly praised for their authenticity, gaiety, and so on, while
Liszt's incomparably more effective use of the same Gypsy
material is condemned as vulgar, meretricious and all the rest
of it. Yet quite apart from Liszt, there is nothing in these pieces
of Brahms to set beside the joy and sadness which Schubert
distilled from Austrian dance music, or to compare with
Chopin's magical transformations of peasant mazurka and

---

* The cymbalom is a large dulcimer used in gypsy bands. The strings,
arranged as in a harp but horizontally, are struck by hammers held in the
player's hands. The instrument originated in the Middle East.

aristocratic polonaise. It is not particularly surprising, despite
the rhythmic interest of the theme, that Brahms's Variations
on a Hungarian Song Op. 21 no. 2 for piano are undistinguished. If he seems to make up for this with the second movement variations on a theme of 'Hungarian' character in his
Piano Trio No. 2 Op. 87 this is due to his finer compositional
technique, not to the alleged 'folk' qualities of the work's
theme.

Brahms's failure to achieve stylistically convincing harmonizations of the few genuine folk melodies which found their
way into the *49 Deutsche Volkslieder* indirectly confirms the
progressive nature of his harmony. This is already suggested
by his links with Wagner and Liszt, who would have had
equally little idea of how to handle such material. As the
ample harmonic colour of a song like *Mein Herz ist schwer*
Op. 94 no. 3 indicates, Brahms cultivated the dense, rich
harmonies of his own time, despite his reputation as a back-
ward-looking conservative, especially in matters of this sort.
On the negative level this might also have stemmed from his
knowledge of Beethoven and his slower harmonies and
Brahms's awareness of his own limitations in the structural
field. Within the German tradition, though, he made some
innovations: with his use of chords on all degrees of the scale
in a given key, not just at cadences, and in exploiting relations
between keys a third apart. At the same time, he was restrained
in his use of keys and individual chords, reserving important
harmonic degrees just as he saves up a telling melody note
until it can have maximum effect.

This drawing of variety from economy obviously parallels
his motivic development of melody. Brahms said to Heuberger
that 'The bass must be a kind of reflection [*Spiegelbild*] of the
upper part', and to Henschel that 'In writing songs one must
endeavour to invent, simultaneously with the melody, a
healthy, powerful bass . . . and no heavy dissonances on the
unaccented parts of the bar. That is weak. I'm very fond of
dissonances, you'll agree, but on the heavy, accented parts of
the bar; and then let them be resolved easily and gently'. The
vitality of his basses, which in his case is a link with the
Baroque, is something we should expect from Brahms's

contrapuntal skill, and partly explains why his chromaticism rarely obscures the tonal centre, as does that of Chopin or Wagner. (To say this is not adversely to criticize these latter masters, whose harmony without question produces exactly the effect they intended.) Nonetheless, we should note the subtly shifting tonality of Brahms's *Liebesklage des Mädchens* Op. 48 no. 3, and the case of *Mondenschein* Op. 85 no. 2, where there is a recitative-like passage of nine bars during which no key centre is properly established, definite tonality only being insisted upon at the words 'ach da fliesst wie stiller Segen'. Again, in *Parole* Op. 7 no. 2 the piano begins apparently in C major, but forms the chord of the augmented sixth on C and moves to the 6/4 of E minor. Several other sorts of ambiguity are exploited, too, as in *Es geht ein Wehen* Op. 62 no. 6, an unaccompanied choral piece in which the basses repeat the third of the minor giving the impression that it is the root of the major.

As we might expect, Schubert is the main influence on Brahms's remoter modulations, but even the simplest key changes are usually made with unaffected individuality. Minor forms of the tonic and sub-dominant were his favoured pivots, and the characteristic dark harmonic colour of this music is due to his liking for sub-dominant harmony—he often returns from dominant harmony via sub-dominant. Brahms's cadences are often worthy of attention, as in *Gestillte Sehnsucht* Op. 91 no. 1, especially at 'Wann schläft ihr, wann schläft ihr ein?' with the beautiful G minor/E minor harmonies, and with the viola taking over the theme from the voice. In Op. 70 no. 1, *Im Garten am Seegestade*, the variety of cadences adds considerably to the effect of an undistinguished melody, and in *Ein Sonett* Op. 14 no. 4 each verse closes with an ardent feminine ending. Also worth noting are *Trennung* Op. 14 no. 5, where a modulation lends a new aspect to the fourth verse, *'Das Scheiden, Scheiden tuet Not'*, the shift to G flat and back in *Dein blaues Auge hält so still* Op. 59 no. 8 and the effect of the modulation at *'Dräuen gleich'* in *Treue Liebe dauert lange* Op. 33 no. 15. In *Liebe und Frühling* Op. 3 no. 3 there is a striking move through B major–B minor–B flat minor–B major and in *Feldeinsamkeit* Op. 86 no. 2 a lovely modulation to D flat major and return to C major, brought off so quickly and smoothly.

The rôle of pedal notes also deserves attention, in *Geheimnis* Op. 71 no. 3, in *Es träumte mir, ich sei dir teuer* Op. 57 no. 3, in *Abenddämmerung* Op. 49 no. 5, or in the third movement of the Requiem Op. 45, where a remarkable effect of strength and steadfastness is created. A contrasting instance is the pedal C throughout *Wiegenlied*, no. 11 of the *Volkskinderlieder*, which is reminiscent of the sustained D flat of Liszt's *Berceuse*!

Further examples of Brahms's harmonic skill are *Vorüber* Op. 58 no. 7, where harmonic subtlety does much to prevent the melody from sounding banal, *Wie traulich war das Fleckchen* Op. 63 no. 7, where a rather lightweight accompaniment is given more seriousness through varied harmony, or the grace with which the melody lends itself to transient harmonic inflections in *Treue Liebe* Op. 7 no. 1. However, one should also remember cases like *Ich sah als Knabe Blumen blühn* Op. 63 no. 9, where, in contrast to *Vorüber*, the melody seems unduly controlled by the harmony in a way that one might have thought Brahms would prefer to avoid, or *Feldeinsamkeit* Op. 86 no. 2, where, as previously remarked, the melody has little independent life apart from the accompaniment. The latter is, admittedly, a special instance where the creation of atmosphere overrides other concerns, and in the case, say, of *Über die Heide* (No. 4 of the same opus) although the vocal line does have greater independence the overall effect, though energetic, is somewhat less impressive.

The expressive effect of these emphases is sometimes quite direct, as in the rather uninteresting *Vergebliches Ständchen* Op. 84 no. 4 where the second verse begins in the minor, reflecting the lover's disappointment. This is also exemplified in the preceding song of Op. 84, *In den Beeren*, in the move to E flat minor, then to B major when the daughter comes in, in the quaver accompaniment at her first mention of the beloved and in the abrupt yet perfectly convincing return to a bright E flat major. Notice also in *Blinde Kuh* Op. 58 no. 1 how the harmony gives just the right sort of confused effect, or how in *Mädchenlied* Op. 107 no. 5 although the shift to the major on 'Die Tränen rinnen' seems illogical it is explained at 'Ich weiss es nicht', which not only returns to the minor but emphasizes the sub-dominant to produce that plagal colouring which Brahms liked so much.

Typical though such moments are, nothing in Brahms's musical personality is more distinctive than his rhythms and nothing so quickly separates him from true conservatives such as Dietrich, Götz or Reinecke. These rhythms, as already noted, partly arise, as with Schubert, from his lyricism and specifically from the requirements of setting words. The duet *Klänge* Op. 66 no. 2 is a good example of rhythmic resource imparting character to somewhat neutral material, and *Von waldbekränzter Höhe* Op. 57 no. 1 is even better. In this latter song, rhythmic freedom covers the divisions of Daumer's commonplace lines, and the anticipation and delay of the first and last phrases respectively of verses two and three adds to the variety while increasing the effect of rhapsodic expression.

Brahms's teacher, Marxsen, had placed much emphasis on accurate performance of the cross-rhythms which play a considerable rôle in his own compositions and, arising from this, on the cultivation of the left hand (this latter point being confirmed by his Three Studies for Left Hand Op. 33). Brahms followed him in both these matters, and piano students of his such as Eugenie Schumann and Florence May tell us that he constantly stressed the importance of rhythm—and especially of syncopation in performing his own and other music.

This freedom also resulted in part from his knowledge of Palestrina and other pre-J. S. Bach music for there is often a tendency to rhythmic variety where unaccompanied vocal composition predominates. However, Brahms's main resources came, as we should expect, from within the German tradition itself. By the late eighteenth century such composers had worked out a subtle method of deploying the relatively few rhythmic devices they had, Haydn and Mozart in particular achieving exceptional use of varied phrase-lengths, creating perfectly balanced forms that actually consist of asymmetrical quantities. This was further developed by musicians such as Brahms, leading eventually to the freedom of metre found in Schoenberg's *Erwartung* and *Die glückliche Hand*, Opp. 17 and 18. The freely declamatory style of later Wagner also contributed. The music of Spohr is also relevant. His Symphony No. 4 Op. 86, called *Die Weihe der Töne*, combines 2/8, 3/8 and 9/16 metres simultaneously in its slow movement in a way that clearly owes something to the Act I finale of *Don Giovanni*. A further example is the very frequent syncopation of Dussek's later piano music, such as the last movement to his Op. 61 Sonata, titled *Elégie harmonique*, which arises, like the chromatic harmony, from eighteenth-century *Sturm und Drang* works. Also prophetic of Brahms is the use of hemiola which became widespread during the nineteenth century, most significantly in the works of Weber, Schubert and Schumann. Altogether, Schumann's use not only of hemiola but of syncopation— including of harmonic rhythm, and polyrhythm show him to be a master of rhythm comparable to Berlioz or Stravinsky, and it was surely from him that Brahms learnt most on this aspect of music. There were, however, other rhythmic influences: the Allegretto of Spohr's Quintet Op. 52 breaks up eight-bar periods into three- and five-bar phrases, while in his *Prinz Eugen*, Loewe uses mixed metres. This probably influenced the unexpected bar-groupings in Brahms's *Lied von Shakespeare* (4444552) and *Der Gärtner* (3334334), Op. 17 nos. 2 and 3. Such influences can also be seen in Brahms's duet *Es rauschet das Wasser* Op. 28 no. 3 where special emphasis is given to the man's 'doch bleiben die Sterne' by lengthening from 4/4 into 6/4; further examples are the switch from 3/2 to 4/4 at 'wo ist er nun' in *Der Strom* Op. 32 no. 4 and the 4/4 introduced into the basic 3/4 in *Sehnsucht* Op. 14 no. 8— Brahms wanting the singer to pause for exactly one beat. He also used changes in rhythm to produce an effect of agitation. Examples of this are the 6/4 over 4/4 in *So stehn wir, ich und meine Weide* Op. 32 no. 8 and the 3/8 over 2/4 in *Beim Abschied* Op. 95 no. 3.

Sometimes he uses syncopation to convey this agitation, as in *Wir müssen uns trennen, geliebtes Saitenspiel* Op. 33 no. 8, but it is also used to quite different ends, as in the following lullaby, *Ruhe, Süssliebchen* Op. 33 no. 9. In *An die Nachtigall* Op. 46 no. 4 syncopation adds to the intensity of the harmonic inflections; in *Anklänge* Op. 7 no. 3 the device may seem to be overused—in fact it conveys more than an impression of longing anticipation, for as the girl blithely spins her wedding gown only the unease of the piano's commentary tells us that she will never wear it. Notice also the effect of rhythmically displaced basses in *Ein Wanderer* Op. 106 no. 5 at 'Meiner ist der Weg der Leiden' and then at 'Wo ich einst begraben warde', and the use of syncopation throughout *Nachtwandler* Op. 86 no. 3.

The prevalence in Brahms's music of melodies derived from common chords might so easily have led to banality, yet rhythmic variety often prevents this. *Während des Regens* Op. 58 no. 2, with its 6/4 and 9/4, is a good instance, and it might be pointed out that whereas in *Vergangen ist mir Glück und Heil* Op. 48 no. 6 he has not bothered to bar the music unevenly— as could readily have been done—the eight time changes of the former song are to make the strong beats evident. As usual, precedents for such changes can be found, such as the Schubert *Kriegers Ahnung* D. 957, with its two sections each in 3/4 and 6/8 with one in 4/4. Again, it is typical of Brahms that in *Der Kuss* Op. 19 no. 1 he should choose, perhaps unconsciously, to convey the wonder of the moment caught in Hölty's lines by means of a balance of three-, four- and five-bar phrases; these phrases are in no way implied in the verse metre yet they do not upset it. In *Die Kränze* Op. 46 no. 1, on the other hand, the music's irregular rhythms reflect those of the text, while in the second movement of the Rhapsody Op. 53 mixed rhythms convey a sharp impression of Goethe's wanderer, so heart-broken that he seems almost to stumble. Again, in *Rosmarin* Op. 62 no. 1 the changes from 3/4 to 4/4 effectively coincide with the girl's own statements as distinct from the narrative, and in *Jägerlied* Op. 66 no. 4 at each reply by the huntsman Brahms changes from 2/4 to 6/8 (and from major to minor, the accompaniment shifting, a bit self-consciously, from key-board figuration to canon).

Two further songs provide an interesting comparison. *Frühlingstrost* Op. 63 no. 1 is characterized by rhythmic complications: it is in 6/4 yet the accompaniment is largely in 3/2 and the eagerness of the vocal phrases lead to half-bar anticipations. In contrast, *Walpurgisnacht* Op. 75 no. 4 uses no special rhythmic resources, its excitement arising from the uniform rhythm's building of tension. Other rhythmic devices worthy of note are the unusual feminine endings of *Gang zur Liebsten* Op. 14 no. 6, which gives a deliberately weakened effect to the voice's last syllable despite its falling on a strong beat, the way in *Minnelied* Op. 44 no. 1 all the phrases both start and finish on an unaccented note, and the spontaneous use of 5/4 (3 + 2) in *Mädchenlied* Op. 85 no. 3. This last work has something of the aspect of a Serbian folk song and quin-tuple time, found in folk song from many parts of the world, is almost the only device related to such music that Brahms used virtually with unselfconsciousness. Indeed, 5/4 was perhaps so closely identified with unsophisticated forms of utterance that it could not find favour until the Romantic period with its concern over the past and with new means of expression. However, Handel had used it in *Orlando* to convey agitation and, nearer Brahms's own time, it occurs in the slow movement to Chopin's Piano Sonata No. 1 Op. 4. In *Agnes* Op. 59 no. 5 quintuple time is crossed with five-bar phrases, another favourite device of Brahms's occurring throughout his work. These latter have a precedent not only in, say, Mozart's String Quartet No. 23 K. 590, with the 7 + 7 and 5 + 5 phrases of the Minuet, but, more expectedly, in Schubert with his *Alte Liebe rostet nie* D. 477 and *Grablied* D. 218. Among the more interesting Brahms examples are *Vom verwundeten Knaben* Op. 14 no. 2 with its seven verses each of two five-bar phrases, *Am Sonntag Morgen* Op. 49 no. 1, where the five feet of Heyse's lines are matched with five-bar phrases, *Nächtens* Op. 112 no. 2, an interesting vocal equivalent to the late keyboard intermezzos—and, of course, the main thematic phrases of the Haydn Variations Op. 56, instantly contrasted though they are with a conventional 4 + 4!

With some Brahms *Lieder*, such as *In der Gasse* Op. 58 no. 6 or *Klosterfräulein* Op. 61 no. 2, we find three-bar vocal phrases with a single piano bar added to make up a four-bar unit, while the five-bar phrases ending the first and second stanzas of *Dämmrung senkte sich von oben* Op. 59 no. 1 are in effect written-out *rallentandos*. Büssler's dictum that 'The greatest masters of form prefer free and bold constructions to being confined within even-numbered bar groups' is affirmed by Brahms, even if one does not rank him among the 'greatest masters of form'. Even so, his relative lack of interest in word-painting—compared with Schubert or Wolf—and his concern with motivic development, led him at times to sacrifice correct declamation of the text to the requirements of melodic flow. Yet repeatedly setting the same brief German verses did lead even the greatest composers to undue similarities of phraseology, even though it might at one time have been fashionable to explain cases like the following, from Schubert's *Die schöne Müllerin* D. 795, as 'proving' the 'unity' of the cycle:

Further examples can easily be found in the work of all the *Lieder* composers, though because of the extensive revision which his songs underwent they are fewer in Brahms than elsewhere. Also, his contrapuntal skill, while immediately apparent in only a few of his *Lieder*, helped to increase the length of his lines and freedom of rhythm in a way that is particularly noticeable in a period so concerned with harmonic exploration and local idioms. Even with Brahms, in, say, *Ach wende diesen Blick* Op. 57 no. 4, the rich harmony gives an undue heaviness to the central verse, though in *Wenn du nur zuweilen lächelst*, No. 2 of that same group—which has both rhythmic and harmonic variety—the accompaniment allows the latter to unfold without turgidity. The middle section of *Alte Liebe* Op. 72 no. 1, however, shows the various elements working particularly well together, the harmonic inflections allied to a continual *accelerando* leaving us scarcely aware that there is little melody in the obvious sense.

Generally these accompaniments diverge from the usual nineteenth-century tendency of giving the piano progressively more prominence—something which began with Schubert and was encouraged by Romantic keyboard virtuosity. Indeed, arpeggio formulae predominate rather too heavily in many Brahms accompaniments, and although the result is good in, for example, the harp-like support to the vocal line of *Es träumte mir, ich sei dir teuer* Op. 57 no. 3, more often the effect is too neutral. And though, again, there are exceptions, such as *Der Schmied* Op. 19 no. 4, a combination of arpeggio figures in both voice and keyboard parts gives insufficient contrast. Sometimes, as in *Ständchen* Op. 14 no. 7, a very simple accompaniment—in this case deriving most of its interest from the harmony—is enough, and like the brevity of *Ich schleich' umher betrübt und stumm* Op. 32 no. 3 or *Gold überwiegt die Liebe* Op. 48 no. 4, indicates Brahms's characteristic desire for concentration, which led him to avoid the many preludes, interludes and postludes found in Schumann's *Lieder*. Naturally there are a considerable number of exceptions in a published output of about two hundred songs, and a few pieces such as *Abschied* and *Tambourliedchen* Op. 69 nos. 3 and 5 have preludes, interludes and postludes. Also notable in effect are the preludes of *In der Fremde* Op. 3 no. 5 and *Heimkehr* Op. 7 no. 6, the interludes of *Traun! Bogen und Pfeil sind gut für den Feind* Op. 33 no. 2 and *An ein Veilchen* Op. 49 no. 2, and the postludes of *Ständchen* Op. 14 no. 7 and *Erinnerung* Op. 63 no. 2.

Brahms's ideal was represented by an accompaniment such as that to Schubert's *Auf der Donau* D. 553, which immediately reaches the heart of the matter. It follows that although plenty of instances may be found in Brahms where the piano imitates details of the text—such as the pairs of quavers suggestive of falling tears in *Die Kränze* Op. 46 no. 1, the hint of a laugh in the accompaniment to *Vergebliches Ständchen* Op. 84 no. 4, or the spinning-wheel of *Mädchenlied* Op. 107 no. 5—it is more characteristic of the composer that only in the first two *Magelone Romanzen* does the piano sound any chivalric overtones, and elsewhere in that cycle (the lute echoed in Nos. 3 and 8 notwithstanding) picturesque details are not enforced.

Yet the texts are sometimes mirrored vividly, as in *Edward* Op. 75 no. 1 when Edward confesses the crime and the whole accompaniment changes except the rhythm (the key shifting from F minor to D flat major in a way comparable to the move from E flat to B major of *In den Beeren* Op. 84 no. 3), or, more negatively, the way in *Traun! Bogen und Pfeil sind gut für den Feind* Op. 33 no. 2 Peter's impetuosity in setting off on his adventures is emphasized by the absence of any keyboard prelude at all. Again, in *Wehe, so willst du mich wieder, hemmende Fessel* Op. 32 no. 5 the restlessness of Platen's verses is conveyed chiefly through the flexible accompaniment's bold harmonic inflections, while in *Wir wandelten* Op. 96 no. 2 a figure of off-beat single notes is spun into an evocation of the bells mentioned by Daumer's poem.

More typical of Brahms, though, is the deft semiquaver dispersal of two-part harmony in *Lied* Op. 3 no. 6, the novel rhythmic distribution of the left-hand notes in verses 1, 3 and 5 of *Frühlingstrost* Op. 63 no. 1, or the way the bass strengthens the effect of the melody without actually duplicating it at the close of *Meine Lieder* Op. 106 no. 4. It is instructive to compare the keyboard part of *Wie soll ich die Freude, die Wonne denn tragen* Op. 33 no. 6, an ecstatic Allegro, with that of Schubert's *Mein* from *Die schöne Müllerin* D. 795: the older composer builds up a vigorous dance over a sturdy yet inactive bass while Brahms uses a more active bass and his characteristic mixed rhythms to convey excitement.

It seems remarkable that Schumann the publisher's son, growing up surrounded by books, and not Brahms, gave more prominence to the piano than to the voice, but in fact he was too introspective to enter completely into any poet's thought, even that of Heine with whom he had so much in common, and his chosen verses are the starting point of an entirely personal meditation. Certainly in *Dichterliebe* Op. 48 the main interest lies with the keyboard, despite Heine's texts, and though in Brahms the emphasis is so often on the voice for him also the poem was chiefly a stimulus to compose rather than an object of psychological interest in itself, as it was to Schubert or Wolf. Naturally there are exceptions to this such as *Nachtwandler* Op. 86 no. 3, where at the close the piano has more of the heart of the matter than the voice, the fourteen-bar opening solo which sets the mood for *Meerfahrt* Op. 96 no. 4, and the concluding solo of *An den Mond* Op. 71 no. 2. A special case is *An die Stolze* Op. 107 no. 1, where, even more than in *An ein Bild* Op. 63 no. 3, the keyboard part is the musical basis of the whole piece, written almost in organ style, a two-bar motive being worked throughout in such a way as almost to reduce the vocal line to a counter-melody.

Although such instances are few among Brahms's *Lieder*, this growing importance of the accompaniment in nineteenth-century song is confirmed by works quite different from his, such as Rimsky-Korsakov's early 'In the dark grove'. This led first to Wolf being virtually forced to orchestrate some of his *Lieder*, then not only to cycles like Schoenberg's Opp. 8 and 22, which have full orchestral accompaniment, but also to works by Ravel, Webern, Stravinsky and others in which the voice is supported by a chamber ensemble. Schumann accorded great prominence to the keyboard but this is somewhat paradoxical in the case of Wolf, for whom the poet was supreme, although the tendency is one that goes back a comparatively long way in the history of the *Lied*. Thus while Schubert's finest songs hold all elements perfectly in balance and unlike Brahms's *Lieder* are rich in psychological as well as musical insights, he also contemplated larger canvases, the first draft of his 1814 *Szene aus Faust* D. 126 being apparently intended for soloists, chorus and orchestra. That his songs are well suited to instrumental textures is also suggested by the fact that the second Trio of his familiar Entr'acte in B flat for *Rosamunde* is an orchestration of *Die Leidende* D. 207, and it is interesting to recall his orchestration and considerable improvement of Stadler's *Unendlicher Gott*. Brahms's orchestrations of Schubert songs are generally inferior in imaginative quality to those of Liszt, but an exception is *Ellens Gesang II* D. 838, which he scored most effectively for soprano soloist, SSA chorus, four horns and two bassoons.

Although, aside from the *Magelone Romanzen* Op. 33, there is nothing in his output on the scale of, say, Goethe's *Prometheus*, with which both Schubert and Wolf were so successful, Brahms's last songs, the *Vier ernste Gesänge* Op. 121, do break the bounds of the *Lied*—even if in a way quite different from Wolf, Mahler or Schoenberg. It is possible that if he had lived longer Brahms might have composed more elaborate settings comparable to theirs, even if the general tendency of his earlier work is in another direction. Certainly there are scattered hints of this in his accompaniments, such as the violin and harp writing suggested by the introduction of *Wie bist du, meine Königin* Op. 32 no. 9, the cello-like melody in the keyboard part of *Abenddämmerung* Op. 49 no. 5, or, much earlier, the left-hand viola phrases on the last page of *Nachtigallen schwingen* Op. 6 no. 6. *Frühlingslied* Op. 85 no. 5 also has an instrumental rather than pianistic character and there is a suggestion of trombone scoring in the accompaniment to *Verrat* Op. 105 no. 5.

These tendencies notwithstanding, some of Brahms's early vocal music does make a rather negative impression—like his orchestral Serenades Opp. 11 and 16. No doubt this is partly because, like Beethoven, he was discontented with the formulae of vocal writing and word-setting that he had inherited—despite the admiration they shared for Handel. The excessive repetitions of the words in *Juchhe!* Op. 6 no. 4 or the awkward soprano line in parts of Psalm XIII Op. 27 reflect Brahms's dissatisfaction and are the kind of weaknesses that were perhaps inevitable until he had found his own way. But he remained unduly modest about his achievements in this field, telling his pupil Jenner that he liked his *Strophenlieder* and other small songs best. A few of his less interesting *Lieder* are simple strophic pieces with the identical music repeated to serve each verse, such as *Gang zur Liebsten* Op. 14 no. 6 or *Trost in Tränen* Op. 48 no. 5, but, with his fertility of invention, Brahms more often went for variants of this. In *Vom verwundeten Knaben* Op. 14 no. 2, for example, verses 1, 2, 3 and 7 have the same music but 4 shifts to the relative major, 5 to the relative major of the sub-dominant and 6 from the sub-dominant back to the original key. *Mit vierzig Jahren* Op. 94 no. 1 follows another path, varying the strophic pattern in accord with the sense of Rückert's verses. In *Spanisches Lied* Op. 6 no. 1 verses 1 and 5, in A minor, are the same, 2 and 4, in E major, are shorter and bolder, while 3 is a variant of 1 and 5.

The strophics of Op. 69 are diverse in size and approach, ranging from the expansive *Vom Strande*, No. 6, to the concise simplicity of *Über die See*, No. 7, while *Mädchenfluch*, No. 9, anticipates the swiftly changing moods of the *Zigeunerlieder* Op. 103. By this time, however, strophic songs were rare, and more to be expected were pieces like *Die Spröde* Op. 58 no. 3, where the music changes, and most tellingly, for the last verse, or *Agnes* Op. 59 no. 5, in which the accompaniment is varied with each stanza. No. 1 of Opus 59, *Dämmrung senkte sich von oben*, marks an interesting stage between a *Strophenlied* and a *durchkomponiert* piece: Goethe's poem has four verses and the music of the second begins like the first, though with a different accompaniment; in the second half this process is reversed, the melody being varied while the accompaniment of the first stanza is resumed; then two verses are combined in one setting in a way that recalls *In meiner Nächte Sehnen* Op. 57 no. 5; key and rhythm change, and neutral diminished seventh harmony takes us to the dominant in preparation for the final verse; but for a whole phrase the music hovers between major and minor, only settling in the fifth bar of this final verse. This meeting of two song-types is, of course, typical of so many aspects of Brahms's art, as is his desire to achieve balance within an opus by mixing the various forms and levels of expression together. With Op. 43, for instance, we find juxtaposed *Ich schell mein Horn ins Jammertal*, No. 3, a simple strophic piece, *Die Mainacht*, No. 2, an example of something like *Magelone* luxuriance, and *Von ewiger Liebe*, No. 1, a return to the rather confined sternness of most of the Op. 32 set.

Even such *Lieder* as *Feldeinsamkeit* Op. 86 no. 2 or *Sapphische Ode* Op. 94 no. 4 retain a strophic framework, and, according to Jenner, Brahms's first question about a song was whether its musical form corresponded to that of the text. From such a principle arose the variety of approaches he adopted, despite the fact that he was sometimes careless of the correct stress of the poet's lines. Even in his justly famous *Die Mainacht* Op. 43 no. 2, for example, because the composer was thinking of the beauty of his melody rather than of Hölty's equally beautiful words, there is undue stress on '*wann*' and '*durch*':

Many other examples of awkward setting could be found, as at the beginning of *An den Mond* Op. 71 no. 2 or near the close of *Geheimnis* Op. 71 no. 3. In view of these and similar instances it is rather surprising (again according to Jenner) that Brahms attached such importance to the pause, recommending a composer frequently to recite a poem aloud before setting it, so as to be sure of the natural separations, the points at which the piano could take over. Similarly, cadences received close attention so that the degree of conclusion in the musical sense should precisely accord with that of the text's literary punctuation. Although in some instances, such as Op. 64 no. 1, a whole song appears to have grown from a single line or word, in this case '*Heimat*', and though in, say, *Der Tod, das ist die kühle Nacht* Op. 96 no. 1 every nuance of Heine's verses is followed by the music, it is difficult—as with Schumann—to feel that Brahms always followed his own precepts. His insistence on firm outlines, again reported by Jenner, is more consistently reflected in his work, in particular his practice when examining a new song of covering up the right hand of the keyboard part and looking only at the melody and bass.

However, there is no denying the fact that *Schön war, das ich dir weihte* Op. 95 no. 7 is a bad setting; its music simply does not fit the construction of the poem. Daumer's rhymes, such as *beide/Geschmeide* or *gewesen/auserlesen*, come in the middle of Brahms's musical phrases, and according to him *auserlesen* ought to rhyme with *Geschmeide*. Each should have a further syllable on the E natural, as at the close of the song—*bessern Lohn*—with an accent on the final syllable. This whole piece, as Drinker has said, 'must be sung with flagrant disregard of the construction of the German poem'. Again, the song we know as *Nachtigall* Op. 97 no. 1 was originally a setting of an entirely different poem which Brahms used again in *Ein Wanderer* Op. 106 no. 5, and it is hard to believe that the Op. 97 melody would be equally suitable for two such different sets of verses.

Long before Brahms's time German composers had proved themselves slow in acknowledging correct principles of declamation, as may be seen by comparing, for example, Schütz and J. S. Bach with Byrd and Purcell. A parallel kind of insensitivity to words is apparent in *Meerfahrt* Op. 96 no. 4 where Brahms's barcarolle-type response (pushed to slightly undue complication for Reinhold's less sophisticated words to *Auf dem See* Op. 106 no. 2) is used too literally for Heine, a poet noted for his subtlety. Surely what he means to tell us in *Meerfahrt* is that the couple are uncertain of how to act, they are 'at sea' in the metaphorical sense. Little confirmation here of Schopenhauer's view that in a song the music's content becomes the image of the poet's idea! Nor does it make much sense in the fifth movement of the Requiem Op. 45 to have the soprano singing 'Und eure Freude soll niemand von euch nehmen'* at the same time that the chorus has 'Ich will euch trösten wie einen seine Mutter tröstet'.** And though the case of *Von ewiger Liebe* Op. 43 no. 1 (which uses material from an early unpublished bridal chorus) has already been cited as an instance of his skill in re-working old material for new purposes (see Ex. p. 78), we may well ask again if the same melody can really be suitable for two such

---

* 'And your joy no man taketh from you.'
** 'I will comfort you as a man's mother comforts him.'

different texts. Similarly, the music of *Klage* Op. 69 no. 2 seems curiously calm beside Wenzig's poem; and that Brahms himself was not always satisfied is suggested by his description of *Die Schale der Vergessenheit* Op. 46 no. 3 as dry and worthless, and by his unwillingness to publish this song. It is also hard to justify his response to Hölderlin in the *Schicksalslied* Op. 54 (despite the purely musical precedents in Mozart and Beethoven mentioned above), or at least to understand his repeat of the celestial prelude material at the close, as this flatly contradicts the stark contrast with which the poet leaves us.

A case like the *Schicksalslied* cannot be justified by any blithe talk of ternary form, and ultimately, as Brahms rightly implied, a misconception of the chosen text will produce an unsatisfying musical structure. There is poor workmanship, for example, in *Nachwirkung* Op. 6 no. 3, despite the interludes built on the theme in diminution, and in *Heimkehr* Op. 7 no. 6, which, its passionate declamation notwithstanding, does not sufficiently develop its material. *Weg der Liebe* Op. 20 no. 2, despite the smooth handling of contrary motion between voices and piano already noted, is unimaginative, with its 4+4 phrases, the voices too consistently in thirds and sixths, the accompaniment heavy; even the coda is four bars. A different case is *Der Frühling* Op. 6 no. 2, which early won praise for its adept use of stock-in-trade procedures, its passages in sequence and its graceful progressions, yet which really should be set beside Schubert's *Heimliches Lieben* D. 922, an example of drawing-room—or at least *Biedermeier*—Schubert.

There are few signs of purely verbal cleverness in Brahms's *Lieder*, despite the word-play on *Flasche* and *falsche* in *Unüberwindlich* Op. 72 no. 5 or between *An's Auge* and *Ansauge* in *An's Auge des Liebsten* Op. 113 no. 9, but he was prepared to make adjustments concerning the exact emphasis of a word, as when, following criticism by Elisabet von Herzogenberg, he lengthened the final verse of *Entführung* Op. 97 no. 3 by one bar to give added point to the climax. *Ein Wanderer* Op. 106 no. 5, Brahms's second attempt to set this poem, was re-cast following extensive adverse comments from the same source, yet he appears to have been unmoved by her rather just remark on *Auf dem See* Op. 106 no. 2 that 'I should visualize "ein schwimmend Eden" as less bristling, and without this array of obstacles in the harmony'. *Liebe und Frühling* Op. 3 no. 2, on the other hand, has the kind of self-consciousness found almost exclusively in Brahms's early songs, its contrapuntal ingenuities being imposed upon Hoffmann von Fallersleben's simple verses, not arising from them.

However, the first song of his earliest set, *Liebestreu* Op. 3 no. 1 is a very good instance of a poem effectively shaping a song's form. The singer's exhortations grow in vehemence in Brahms's setting while the first two answers remain placid; the suitability of these verses for musical treatment lies partly in the fact that the third reply responds to the force generated by the overall *accelerando* and *crescendo* so that the climax arises naturally and is most effectively placed. Note also the change to the tonic major for the third verse and the quasi-12/8 of constant triplets in the right hand against straight crotchets and quavers in the left, producing an *agitato* perfectly apt for Reinick's poem. *In der Fremde* and *Lied*, Nos. 5 and 6 of Op. 3, are also of interest; the first seems to be *durchkomponiert* yet is actually divided into two sections that differ in small yet telling ways; the second song is in three parts, the last an exultant condensation of the first. *Vor dem Fenster* Op. 14 no. 1 is another good example of Brahms's music reflecting the wayward character of a poem; in the fourth verse, the effect of a shift to the major and of the voice part going up in register is like the sun breaking through clouds, a contrast typical of the composer—and most unlike the folk music that this and the other Op. 14 settings are supposed to emulate.

There are other points worth noting which concern the shaping of these *Lieder* in accord with their poems. In *Minnelied* Op. 71 no. 5, for example, the ternary form of this melodious and tender song is skilfully disguised. (Although the music is in ternary form, the poem is not, so Brahms disguises the ternary aspect to place the music more in line with the poem.) A further example is *Treue Liebe dauert lange* Op. 33 no. 15 where constancy is praised on a return to the first theme. More generally, in his song *Strahlt zuweilen auch ein mildes Licht* Op. 57 no. 6 Brahms vividly catches the fleeting impression of Daumer's poem. Close examination proves this last and many other songs of similar quality to be more elaborate in their organization than a casual hearing would suggest, and the following break-down of *Regenlied* Op. 59 no. 3 may give some idea of the care with which Brahms produced his effects, drawing musical poetry from quite unremarkable verses—in this case by Klaus Groth:

(i) 4 bars (2 + 2) piano introduction;

(ii) *First verse* of 16 bars (2 + 2 3 + 1 3 + 1 3 + 1), these 3 + 1 groups indicate three vocal bars plus one from the keyboard, these making up a four-bar phrase;

(iii) 4 bars (2 + 2) piano interlude;

(iv) *Second verse* of 21 bars, the first half exactly the same as the first verse, rhythm exactly the same apart from extension of the last phrase to repeat the final words;

(v) *Third verse* of 8 bars, a remarkable condensation but actually part of a continuous setting with Groth's fourth verse, the two making a coda-like end to what may be considered the song's first movement;

(vi) *Fourth verse* of 15 bars;

(vii) 2 bars piano interlude leading from 4/4 to 3/2;

(viii) *Fifth verse* of 8 bars;

(ix) 2 bars piano interlude;

(x) *Sixth verse* of 11 bars, the same as fifth verse except for necessary changes to revert to 4/4;

(xi) 4 bars piano interlude;

(xii) *Seventh verse* of 16 bars, a recapitulation—the same music as for the first verse;

(xiii) 4 bars piano interlude (the same as the introduction (i));

(xiv) *Eighth verse* of 23 bars, beginning the same as first verse but flowing into broader conclusion;

(xv) 9 bars of piano coda.

As already noted, there was a long tradition of bad word-setting before Brahms; examples from Marschner, Weber and even Mendelssohn—all of them educated men—would prove this. The trouble sprang, especially in Germany, from the common practice dating back to Luther's time of setting new words to old melodies without anyone bothering whether the two fitted sensibly. Also, the singing of different verses of a poem to the same melody led to incongruities, whether in the ballads of Zelter and Zumsteeg or in the *Strophenlieder* of Brahms. Schumann, despite his introspective attitude to poems, was among the first to concern himself over this, and Mendelssohn, following his teacher Zelter, was much inferior—as his *Frühlingsmächtig* Op. 47 no. 3 shows. True, the melodies of certain of his *Lieder* such as *Auf Flügeln des Gesanges* Op. 34 no. 2, a Heine setting, well express the moods of their poems, yet Brahms, profiting to some degree from Schumann's example, often produced superior results. Spitta well realized this when he compared his reaction to Goethe's *Die Liebende schreibt* (Op. 47 no. 5) with Mendelssohn's (Op. 86 no. 3) in a letter to Brahms: 'The poem, with its interlinking of corresponding verses, is musical in itself and should respond to musical treatment. You have succeeded so well that, even in the text's absence, an expert would, I think, be able to recognize the sonnet form. Where Mendelssohn only reflected the elements of the poem and entirely ignored its shape, you have cast a light and graceful garment over it, through which the structure may clearly be seen. And so by adhering to the literary form your piece is the antithesis of that of Mendelssohn.' (Both these settings, of course, should be compared with Schubert's—D. 673.)

Although, as we have seen, Brahms was at times surprisingly insensitive to words, some of the liberties he took were beneficial, rather like a portrait painter exaggerating a detail better to realize the meaning of the whole. Many problems of word-setting arise, however, from the differing rates of expressiveness of words and music, and also from the fact that poets tend to make their points at the ends of lines—which is not where a composer often wishes to place the climax of a phrase. Regarding such difficulties Brahms songs like *Wie rafft' ich mich auf in der Nacht* Op. 32 no. 1 (Platen) or *Feldeinsamkeit* Op. 86 no. 2 (Allmers) are exceptional unities of musical and literary expression. Nietzsche put forward the idea that a poem set to great music does not make an impression as a poem, and it is obviously true that the effect of a song or an opera is primarily musical, not literary. This is despite the fact that, as we have seen, in good songs like Brahms's *Liebestreu* Op. 3 no. 1 or *Die Liebende schreibt* Op. 47 no. 5 the musical form at least partly derives from the poem. Nietzsche's view, however, contradicts the theories of his one-time idol Wagner, who anyway contradicted himself by composing the *Meistersinger* overture—that is, the music to a considerable part of Act III—before he had written the libretto for that act. Certainly a perfect poem, just because of its completeness, can have little added to it by music. The most suitable verses for a song writer and those which give a composer the finest opportunities, are those leaving gaps in their expressive content, thus allowing a collaboration between words and notes. We may be sure it was the problematical aspects of Goethe's *Rinaldo* text that attracted Brahms—and, in corroboration, it is instructive to compare Shakespeare's originals with Boito's librettos of *Falstaff* and *Otello*, noting what he left out in order to create opportunities for Verdi's music. A poem or other text which attracts a composer suggests to him emotions that are only implicit in it but which he can make explicit with his music—to the extent of his capacities. Note the differences between Franz's rather four-square settings of Mörike or Heine and the more complex reactions of Schumann or Wolf to the same texts. A number of settings of bad verse, on the other hand, like Schumann's *Frauenliebe und -leben* Op. 42, are virtually corrections of the text's deficiencies rather than collaborations. In other cases, such as Butterworth's Housman settings, success is due to words and music being on exactly the same level. Brahms's *Immer leiser wird mein Schlummer* Op. 105 no. 2 is an excellent instance of music reaching heights inaccessible to a minor poet (in this case Lingg).

Anything too highly wrought in a text, too intense or too striking, is disruptive of our attention on the music, but the traditions of classical and Romantic poetry made it fairly easy for many versifiers to achieve formal neatness without sounding an individual voice of their own, and such material often suited composers well. However, it might be added that the passion of superior German poetry, transmitted partly through free rhythms, is hard to communicate in translation. For example, the real effect of Platen's closing words for *Der Strom* Op. 32 no. 4,

> '*Und jener Mensch, der ich gewesen,*
> *Und den ich längst mit einem andern Ich vertauschte,*
> *Wo ist er nun?*'

is not particularly well conveyed by, say:

> That other man who once was I, he
> Who long ago became another 'I' entirely,
> Where is he now?

It might be added that Brahms has been subject to some particularly misleading translations, as in Op. 113 no. 8, whose opening line, 'Ein Gems auf dem Stein', has appeared as 'A gem in the stone' instead of as 'A ram on the height'. And some translations have tried to be too contemporary, as when the 'hundert Taler' of *Guter Rat* Op. 75 no. 2 appeared in one one edition as '$100'!

It is instructive to observe how a composer will sometimes alter the actual form of a poem so that words and music can better make a new whole. A simple yet particularly good example of this is Schubert's re-ordering of Rückert's text for *Du bist die Ruh* D. 776, although it is only rarely that a song illumines every single aspect of a good poem. Occasionally another song, rather than the text, appears to be the starting point, and the relation between Brahms's *Mondnacht* and Schumann's treatment of the same Eichendorff poem (Op. 39 no. 5) suggests this to be an instance. This may well account for Brahms's hesitancy in publishing his setting, and when finally it did appear in 1872 it significantly bore no opus number. (Several other Schumann *Lieder* may perhaps be similarly credited, even when the text is different: compare, for instance, his *Da liegt der Feinde gestreckte Schar* Op. 117 no. 4 with Duparc's *Le manoir de Rosemonde*, or his *Berg' und Burgen* Op. 24 no. 7 with Brahms's *Bei dir sind meine Gedanken* Op. 95 no. 2.) Within the bounds of German song, at least, such correspondences do serve to emphasize the limited melodic vocabulary, already referred to, which arose from composers repeatedly setting the same type of poetry. Thus Schumann's *Aus meinen Tränen spriessen* Op. 48 no. 2 starts with just the same phrase as *Das Geheimnis* D. 793 by Schubert.

Despite *Mondnacht*, such cases are hard to find in Brahms's *Lieder* and usually he avoided such family likenesses with other composers. One is struck, however, by a contrast between the variety of his musical treatments and the fairly restricted emotional range of his songs. It is impossible, surely, to imagine him tackling a subject like *Frauenliebe und -leben*. He set few narrative or dramatic poems, and, as Kelterborn points out, his delineations in song tend more to be sympathetic than realistic. The *Magelone Romanzen* Op. 33 are a partial exception, but the earlier numbers were composed in the summer of 1862 at Münster-am-Stein, near the Ebernburg castle ruins, and this local colour, the atmosphere of the Rhine, perhaps had its effect. But it is difficult to think of other cases.

Another very noticeable contrast is between the literary quality of the texts Brahms chose for many of his big choral works and those for the great majority of his *Lieder*. *Rinaldo* Op. 50, the Rhapsody Op. 53 (both Goethe), *Schicksalslied* Op. 54 (Hölderlin), *Nänie* Op. 82 (Schiller), *Gesang der Parzen* Op. 89 (Goethe) and *Tafellied* Op. 93b (Eichendorff) all show how nobly he could respond to great verse, and one can only speculate on what he might have achieved if, like Wolf, he had confined himself to texts of good quality. Or rather, such pieces make us wonder how his song output might have been different in character—though not necessarily in musical quality—if he had done so, considering his insistence, which admittedly he did not always follow, on letting the musical form arise out of the text. Maybe the thought is an idle one for none of Brahms's *Lied* settings of great poetry ranks with his finest songs. The Goethe items, for example, have a very modest place in his output compared with Schubert.

Brahms, like the other chief *Lieder* composers, set only German verse, or, like Schumann and Wolf, translations into German. The contents of his large and quite valuable library prove that he was acquainted with the best of German poetry, even if he did not choose to set it very often. Brahms published seven Eichendorff, seven Goethe, six Heine, six Ludwig Hölty and three Mörike songs, besides devoting Op. 33 to Tieck's Magelone poems. This hardly compares with Schubert's seventy Goethe settings, his twenty-two of Hölty or forty-two of Schiller, whatever might be said of his supposedly inferior taste. Nor is there anything in Brahms to place beside Schubert's repeated settings of the *Wilhelm Meister* songs between 1815 and 1826; no instance, that is, of texts exerting a continuing fascination resulting in the desire to match them with *exactly* the right music, a willingness to try several times— rather than repeatedly to revise one setting; and this is the opposite of what might be expected from the careful, persistent Brahms and the spontaneous, allegedly careless, Schubert. Still less is there anything in Brahms's life to compare with Berlioz's devotion to Virgil and Shakespeare or Liszt's adherence to Dante and Goethe and the fruitful effect these abiding influences had on their work. That Brahms's attitude to his texts was not without its oddness is suggested by passing remarks in several of his letters. For example, in connection with Op. 104 no. 5 he wrote to Elisabet von Herzogenberg, 'I've been trying my hand at Groth's *Im Herbst*, but it's a difficult thing to tackle—difficult and dull!' Like Fauré, he seems to have been guided not by a poet's stature but by a search for atmosphere, and this in a way is reminiscent of Schumann or Debussy who added titles to their shorter piano works only when composing was over.

Brahms appears to have chosen poems in which he could detect a song lurking behind the often mundane imagery; this feeling might derive from the whole poem, from its idea, its mood, the human emotion it portrayed, the rhythm of the words, the images used, or a combination of these. And a few aberrations aside, it is clear that however dubious their literary quality at least Brahms thought they were good in themselves —that is, not just as a stimulus to composition. 'You've got a fine collection of *poems* there, at any rate', he said of von der Leyen's complete set of his *Lieder* (see Bibliography). Further the manuscript of Ophüls's *Brahms-Texte, Vollständige Samm-lung der von Brahms komponierten und musikalisch bearbeiteten Dichtungen*, published the year of his death, was a great source of pleasure during the composer's final months. Poorly educated in his youth, Brahms, despite his wide reading, had the conventional German taste of his day, and found nothing absurd in the stock responses of his preferred very minor poets. One might still wish that he had enquired a little farther, though, on the occasions he did set good verse. In the case, for example, of *Der Kuss* Op. 19 no. 1 it is unfortunate he did not use Hölty's 1776 original version of this poem instead of Voss's misleading abridgement published in 1804, and a similar comment applies to *Die Schale der Vergessenheit* Op. 46 no. 3, another abbreviated Hölty setting.

Despite such unconcern, Hölty's sweetness, truth of senti-ment and musical purity of form did seem able to inspire Brahms's finest vocal melody—*Die Mainacht* Op. 43 no. 2, *An die Nachtigall* Op. 46 no. 4, *An ein Veilchen* Op. 49 no. 2 etc.— and it was this poet he was apt to mention, in an 1869 letter to Schubring for example, when his literary taste was adversely criticized. *Agnes* Op. 59 no. 5 and particularly *An eine Äolsharfe* Op. 19 no. 5 suggest that Brahms could have got more from

Mörike, a writer of limited range who rejected large themes but whose use of classical models contrasted effectively with his melodious accounts of nature and country life. Others, such as Rückert or Uhland he set from time to time, but without evidence of any strong regard, though his attention may have been drawn to the latter by Schumann's Op. 145.

In no sense a regional artist, Brahms was in many ways a typical Low German, and one regrets that he did not more often set poets from his own part of Germany—not just Hebbel (two *Lieder* settings) and Storm (only one), but also Geibel (three), Liliencron (two) and Allmers (one). His music centres round types of expression very similar indeed to those found in their poetry, and they might have given him much. This is proved on the few occasions he did turn to such verse, the vocal quartets *Spätherbst* and *Abendlied* Op. 92 nos. 2 and 3 being acutely responsive to Allmers's and Hebbel's nature evocations, and the late keyboard intermezzos having an atmosphere very close to that of Storm's poetry.

Apart from Daumer (nineteen *Lieder* settings), whose verse sometimes produced a curiously Wagnerian (or at least *Meistersinger*) response from Brahms—as at 'mit Macht im Fliederbusche schlägt die Nachtigall' in *O schöne Nacht* Op. 92 no. 1—his 'statistical' favourite was Groth (thirteen solo settings). This was the one instance of his resorting at all often to a regional poet, but seems to have been due to their personal friendship. All the same, in his 1853 collection of lyric verse, *Quickborn*, Groth appears almost the archetype of the regional poet of his time and place, with dialect relating his work to colloquial speech and his roots in genuine folk verse.

However, most of Brahms's *Lieder* are love songs, as are Schumann's—even though in a sense he had less reason for composing them, there being no event in his life which opened the flood-gates as Schumann's marriage did in 1840. But love, as usual, takes many forms, direct declarations being quite numerous, including *Liebe und Frühling* Op. 3 no. 2, *Ständchen* Op. 14 no. 7, *O liebliche Wangen* Op. 47 no. 4 and *Minnelied* Op. 71 no. 5. Indirect statements of love, perhaps surprisingly from this composer, are fewer, though *An ein Veilchen* Op. 49 no. 2 and *Mädchenlied* Op. 95 no. 6 are among these. Laments

117

for lost love form almost the largest category of Brahms's songs, however, and these include *Nachwirkung* Op. 6 no. 3, *Der Strom* Op. 32 no. 4, *Der Überläufer* Op. 48 no. 2 and *Vom Strande* Op. 69 no. 6. In contrast, only two unequivocal celebrations of love consummated can be found—*Spanisches Lied* Op. 6 no. 1 and *Der Kuss* Op. 19 no. 1—but expressions of loneliness or homesickness are virtually as frequent as regrets for lost love, among them being *Volkslied* Op. 7 no. 4, *Schwermut* Op. 58 no. 5, *Klosterfräulein* Op. 61 no. 2 and *Mädchenlied* Op. 85 no. 3. In two songs Op. 63 nos. 7 and 8, both called *Heimweh*, homesickness is linked specifically with nostalgia for the days of childhood. Occasional hope of love in the future— *Unbewegte laue Luft* Op. 57 no. 8 or *Mädchenfluch* Op. 69 no. 9— is more than balanced by nostalgia for love in the past: *Erinnerung* Op. 63 no. 2, *Im Garten am Seegestade* Op. 70 no. 1, *Alte Liebe* Op. 72 no. 1 and *Über die Heide* Op. 86 no. 4. There is, of course, sadness over love deferred—*Die Liebende schreibt* Op. 47 no. 5, *Sehnsucht* Op. 49 no. 3, *Eine gute, gute Nacht* Op. 59 no. 6 or *Immer leiser wird mein Schlummer* Op. 105 no. 2— and over love deferred through absence: *Der Gang zum Liebchen* Op. 48 no. 1, *An ein Bild* Op. 63 no. 3 or *Ade!* Op. 85 no. 4. Yet there are some lovers' conversations, like *Vor der Tür* Op. 28 no. 2 and *So lass uns wandern* Op. 75 no. 3, and quite a few celebrations of the beloved's attributes, such as *Magyarisch* Op. 46 no. 2, *Dein blaues Auge hält so still* Op. 59 no. 8 or *Tambourliedchen* Op. 69 no. 5. In a number of Brahms songs love is related to other natural phenomena, examples being *Die Mainacht* Op. 43 no. 2, *Liebesklage des Mädchens* Op. 48 no. 3, *Frühlingstrost* and *Meine Liebe* Op. 63 nos. 1 and 5, while in *Wehe, so willst du mich wieder, hemmende Fessel* Op. 32 no. 5 some of the more spectacular aspects of nature are recommended, without much confidence, as a cure for love. There are songs of reproach, like *Beim Abschied* Op. 95 no. 3 or *An die Stolze* Op. 107 no. 1, while the next item, *Salamander* Op. 107 no. 2, makes an ironical comment on love almost unique in Brahms's *Lieder* and a more optimistic view is taken, with unexpected consistency, in *Sommerabend*, *Der Kranz* and *In den Beeren*, the first three numbers of Op. 84.

On examination, the other subjects of Brahms's *Lieder* appear to have a certain family likeness, an instance being the various kinds of nostalgic expression they contain, such as the nostalgia for childhood of *Regenlied* Op. 59 no. 3 and the third *Heimweh* Op. 63 no. 9, for twilight in *Abenddämmerung* Op. 49 no. 5 or, more grimly, in *Der Tod, das ist die kühle Nacht* Op. 96 no. 1. Related to these are his evocations of a dreamlike state, in *Vorüber* Op. 58 no. 7 or *Meine Lieder* Op. 106 no. 4, the philosophical view of life expressed by *Mit vierzig Jahren* Op. 94 no. 1, and even a nostalgia for death itself in *Klänge* Op. 66 no. 2 or *Gestillte Sehnsucht* Op. 91 no. 1. Note also the idea of melodies arising during reverie or dreams in *Wie Melodien zieht es* Op. 105 no. 1. Another vein is represented by the celebrations of natural beauty in songs like *Auf dem See* Op. 59 no. 2 and the reflections on man in nature, on his unity with it and response to its changes, in *O kühler Wald* Op. 72 no. 3 or *Feldeinsamkeit* Op. 86 no. 2, with a more light-hearted example in *Maienkätzchen* Op. 107 no. 4. Also there are lullabies such as *Geistliches Wiegenlied* Op. 91 no. 2 and the very famous *Wiegenlied* Op. 49 no. 4, a single reference to the supernatural in *Walpurgisnacht* Op. 75 no. 4, and even a drinking song, *Unüberwindlich* Op. 72 no. 5. As noted already, narratives are few, but these include *Vom verwundeten Knaben* Op. 14 no. 2, *Das Lied vom Herrn von Falkenstein* Op. 43 no. 4 and *Verrat* Op. 105 no. 5. There are several hunting songs like *Der Jäger* Op. 95 no. 4, *Der Jäger und sein Liebchen* Op. 28 no. 4, and in *Ich schell mein Horn ins Jammertal* Op. 43 no. 3 it is the hunter himself who sings, while the man in *Der Überläufer* Op. 48 no. 2 reminds us, with his green hat, of *Die schöne Müllerin* D. 795. Altogether there is little detachment here, the *Ständchen* Op. 106 no. 1 presenting the unusual case of a description of a serenade, not just the serenade itself.

Humour can be found in Brahms's *Lieder*, more especially in duets, such as *Vor der Tür* Op. 28 no. 2, *Hüt du dich* Op. 66 no. 5 or *Guter Rat* Op. 75 no. 2, for these are a particularly social form of music-making, yet it must be admitted that gloom is more frequent. This is especially so in his choral pieces, with the unpleasant *Triumphlied* Op. 55 as the exception among large-scale items. Several groups of songs are not really suitable to be performed as wholes because of this all too prevailing sadness. With the exception of its last number, *Heimkehr*, which at least is hopeful, Op. 7 offers sad texts only, this naturally being reflected in the tempo directions, which are confined to *andante, langsam* and *bewegt*. Op. 48 is another discouraging set, only the first piece, *Der Gang zum Liebchen*, with its hope of love deferred, giving any cause for optimism, a point again underlined by the tempo indications, which are mainly *andante, etwas langsam* or *ziemlich langsam*. The eight numbers of Op. 57 make a further gloomy sequence, with relief coming only in the last two items, *Die Schnur, die Perl an Perle* and *Unbewegte laue Luft*, with some possible chance, it seems, of love in the future. Still, *Blinde Kuh* and *Während des Regens* Op. 58 nos. 1 and 2 have an extroversion that is surprising, although the rain of *Regenlied* Op. 59 no. 3 suggests very different images from the Op. 58 no. 2.

Water is more painfully evocative in *Abendregen* Op. 70 no. 4 and especially in *Am Strande* Op. 66 no. 3, and plays a symbolic rôle, not often noticed, in a number of Brahms *Lieder*. Compare, for example, the lake of *Dämmrung senkte sich von oben* Op. 59 no. 1 with the waters of the following *Auf dem See* Op. 59 no. 2, then with the rain of *Nachklang*, No. 4 of the same group. The sea is an image of disturbance in *Verzagen* Op. 72 no. 4 and (at least in the text of) *Meerfahrt* Op. 96 no. 4, as it is at the beginning and end of *Versunken* Op. 86 no. 5 and as is the fountain of *Serenade* Op. 58 no. 8. Yet in *Auf dem See* Op. 106 no. 2 water symbolizes security. Rather different is *Es rauschet das Wasser* Op. 28 no. 3, earliest of Brahms's Goethe settings, which employs images of rushing water and the apparent immobility of the stars to parallel the excitements and the constancy of love; but in *Über die See* Op. 69 no. 7 the sea again stands for separation, and it has a rôle also in *Liebestreu* Op. 3 no. 1, *Treue Liebe* Op. 7 no. 1, *Sehnsucht* Op. 14 no. 8 and *Die Meere* Op. 20 no. 3.

Another curious theme, found in *Magyarisch* Op. 46 no. 2, *Ach wende diesen Blick* Op. 57 no. 4, *Dein blaues Auge hält so still* Op. 59 no. 8 and fleetingly in *Versunken* Op. 86 no. 5, is the expression of fear, almost, of the loved one's eyes. As we should expect from Brahms, several kinds of expression sometimes come together in the same *Lied*, and there is a vein of erotic turmoil amid the peace of nature, typified by items already mentioned, including *Die Meere* Op. 20 no. 3, *Die Mainacht* Op. 43 no. 2, *Unbewegte laue Luft* Op. 57 no. 8 and *Gestillte Sehnsucht* Op. 91 no. 1. Other songs, like *Nachklang* Op. 59

no. 4, *Lerchengesang* Op. 70 no. 2 and *Nachtigall* Op. 97 no. 1, lament the inerradicable follies of the past—even if these are only hinted at. *In der Gasse* Op. 58 no. 6 is perhaps a similar case, though here, as in *Steig auf, geliebter Schatten* Op. 94 no. 2, the shadow invoked reminds us of Schubert's *Der Doppelgänger* D. 957.

Brahms's alterations to the poems he chose for his songs have already been mentioned. At times these seem rather pointless, as in *Lied aus dem Gedicht 'Ivan'* Op. 3 no. 4, where Bodenstedt wrote 'und steigst du herauf' which the composer changed to 'hinauf', or in *Wie die Wolke nach der Sonne* Op. 6 no. 5, where he substituted 'auf die Sonn' for Hoffman von Fallersleben's 'nach der Sonne'. A special case, however, is *Blinde Kuh* Op. 58 no. 1, where, in order to avoid the literal repetitions of the first and third lines of Kopisch's original second verse, he replaces its third and fourth lines with the first two lines of the opening verse. Again, in *Die Spröde*, No. 3 of the same opus, he wanted to do without some of Kopisch's rather facile rhymes, although these appeared in the first edition of this song, and he got Heyse to produce a revision which has been used in all subsequent printings. Sometimes, and particularly in his more youthful *Lieder*, Brahms made rather more extensive changes, such as omitting the whole third verse of Johann Rousseau's poem for *Der Frühling* Op. 6 no. 2, or in the second verse of *Weg der Liebe* Op. 20 no. 1, where he substituted 'In Ritzen, in Falten, wo der Feu'rwurm nicht liegt' for Herder's 'In Ritzen und Spalten, wo die Ameis nicht kriecht', 'In Höhlen, in Spalten' for the poet's 'In Höhlen und Falten' and 'Liebe, sie wird siegen' for 'Liebe, sie wird eingehn'. A rather similar case is the so-called folk poem of *Vor dem Fenster* Op. 14 no. 1, for which his sources appear to have been Arnold's *Deutsche Volkslieder mit Melodien* (Elberfeld, n.d.) and his own publisher Simrock's *Die deutschen Volkslieder* (Frankfurt, 1851). These have the same text, from which Brahms made repeated small departures: 'gehn' instead of 'gahn' in the first verse, 'feins Lieb' instead of 'Herzlieb' and 'aus schöner, aus heller Stimme' in place of 'aus schöner, heller Stimme' in the second verse; 'Hörnelein' instead of 'Hörnlein' in the fifth, and 'meinem jungen Herzen' instead of 'einem' and 'nimmermehr' in place of 'nimmermeh'' in the sixth verse. Quite different is the case of *Von wald-bekräntzer Höhe* Op. 57 no. 1, which he wanted to begin with the words 'Von Dornbachs schöner Höhe' as a compliment to the Viennese suburb of Dornbach, but out of undue respect for Daumer's verses he decided to retain the original.

Over the years Brahms's attitude to the poems he set inevitably changed, and this is evident in the altered emphases of early and late songs. In *Der Schmied* Op. 19 no. 4 of 1858, for example, we hear the smith at work, with rather too obvious imitations of his hammer—usually too fast, Brahms's *allegro* being a mistake. But in, say, *Mädchenlied* Op. 95 no. 6, published in 1884, there is no stress on the girl's work, only on the thought of her beloved in Paradise. Brahms's range, although narrower than that of Schubert or Wolf, was actually a bit wider than is sometimes imagined—as a boisterous, convivial piece like *Unüberwindlich* Op. 72 no. 5, with its pointed interruptions and abrupt contrasts in the accompaniment, or the Viennese geniality of *Komm bald* Op. 97 no. 5 may suggest. Yet a *Lied* such as *Abenddämmerung* Op. 49 no. 5, a lengthy meditation of which he was very fond, remains more typical of Brahms, and almost until the end his most characteristic writing in this form occurs when love takes on a sombre, even tragic aspect, when man and nature are fused, or when past sorrows rise up in the memory. He became a master in the expression of resignation and, from either the musical or the spiritual viewpoint, nobody else could have composed *An eine Äolsharfe* Op. 19 no. 5, *Von ewiger Liebe* and *Die Mainacht* Op. 43 nos. 1 and 2, *An die Nachtigall* Op. 46 no. 4, *Herbstgefühl* Op. 48 no. 7, *Unbewegte laue Luft* Op. 57 no. 8, *Alte Liebe* Op. 72 no. 1, *Feldeinsamkeit* and *Todessehnen* Op. 86 nos. 2 and 6 or *Auf dem Kirchhofe* Op. 105 no. 4.

Serious though all these *Lieder* essentially are, there are no instances in Brahms, not even in the *Vier ernste Gesänge* Op. 121, of the black, Dostoievskian introspection found in, say, Mussorgsky's *Without Sunlight* cycle (still less, of course, of his empirical use of dissonance!). And though in a song like *Verrat* Op. 105 no. 5 the singer must obviously distinguish between the man describing the scene and the girl saying farewell to her other lover, there is nothing like the sharp characterization of Mussorgsky's *Songs and Dances of Death*—in, say, the *Cradle Song* between Death and the mother fighting for her sick child. The choral pieces Op. 17 and the songs with viola obbligato Op. 91 may be taken as very tentative dividing-lines between spring, summer and autumn. The two viola *Lieder* actually were composed in 1884–5, but autumn had been heralded, around 1880, by the composer's increasing attraction to the dark tones of a low voice, and though, unlike Robert Franz with his abiding preference for the mezzo-soprano, Brahms had not previously shown any especial predilection, he latterly published several groups of songs '*für eine tiefere Stimme*'.

There is no winter in Brahms's music, unlike that of Schumann or Wolf, his predecessor and successor in the world of the *Lied*, and this despite Billroth's description of Op. 57 as 'A sort of autumn or winter journey'. Yet isolated hints of deep midwinter can be found. Normally, as we have seen, he prefers to follow the general emotional content of a poem, rarely accenting a particular word with an elaborate, aria-like phrase in the manner, say, of Bach. But there is an exception, and that is the idea of death. See how strikingly it is accented in the third of the *Vier ernste Gesänge* Op. 121:

Rather consistently, however, Brahms associates death with thirds, sometimes ascending:

but more usually descending:

In the second of the *Vier ernste Gesänge* a mention of the dead reduces both voice and accompaniment to almost nothing but thirds, mainly descending:

Sometimes death or the dead are not specifically mentioned, and in, of all things, *Feldeinsamkeit* Op. 86 no. 2 the words 'mir ist als ob ich längst gestorben bin' are enough to drive away the accompaniment's solidly rooted basses and continuous right-hand textures as, for a moment, everything becomes detached and descending thirds:

For all their consistency, such features are rare in Brahms's *Lieder*, yet just as we should be aware of certain recurring 'types', like his rain songs—*Während des Regens* Op. 58 no. 2, *Regenlied* and *Nachklang* Op. 59 nos. 3 and 4, *Abendregen* Op. 70 no. 4, etc.—or his nocturnes—*Von ewiger Liebe* Op. 43 no. 1,

Dämmrung senkte sich von oben Op. 59 no. 1, etc.—so we ought to recognize various cross-references beside those noted on earlier pages. Instances are these two passages from *Von wald-bekränzter Höhe* and *Die Schnur, die Perl an Perle*, Op. 57 nos. 1 and 7:

Links between *Sommerabend* and *Mondenschein* Op. 85 nos. 1 and 2 were referred to on page 72, but in the passages where the songs use the identical melody it is worth noting the differences and similarities of Brahms's accompaniments:

Other links could be cited between pairs of *Lieder*, such as the closing bars of *In Waldeseinsamkeit* Op. 85 no. 6 and those of *Es schauen die Blumen* Op. 96 no. 3, which, like the Exs. from Op. 57, illustrate not a constant response to a particular concept in the form of a specific musical element (as in Exs. pp. 123–4) but the composer's power of drawing fresh results from what is basically the same melodic idea.

The close-knit character of the German musical tradition was such that some of the ideas thus varied did not originate with Brahms and were common property. As we have repeatedly seen on earlier pages, many links can be pointed out between his songs, early and late, and those of other composers. Brahms, we may feel sure, was in most instances unaware of these echoes (particularly in the case of *Die Mainacht* Op. 43 no. 2, which has similarities with a Ukrainian folk melody used by Rimsky-Korsakov in his opera *May Night!*). Less exotic from the German viewpoint are *Im Garten am Seegestade* and *Lerchengesang* Op. 70 nos. 1 and 2, with their marked reminiscences of Schumann's *Dichterliebe* cycle Op. 48. There are also references to Schumann at the beginning and end of Brahms's *Magelone Romanzen* Op. 33: to his *Talismane* Op. 25 no. 8 in No. 1, *Keinen hat es noch gereut*, and to the piano suite *Davidsbündlertänze* Op. 6 in *Treue Liebe dauert lange*, No. 15. Schumann, and *Dichterliebe*, again appear in Brahms's *Vom Strande* Op. 69 no. 6, where the accompaniment at 'Vom Strande, lieb Mutter, wo der Wellenschlag geht' and at 'Verhielt ich die Klagen' recalls that of *Das ist ein Flöten und Geigen*, No. 9 of *Dichterliebe*.

Schubert, of course, is even more of a presence in Brahms's music—not only in his *Lieder*. In *Rinaldo* Op. 50, for example, the hero's first solo, especially around 'Stelle her der gold'nen Tage', is very Schubertian in some respects, and at one point the older man's *Am See* D. 746 is nearly quoted. Nor is it only Schubert's vocal works that cast their shadow. In *An den Mond* Op. 71 no. 2 the keyboard part at 'Sag ihr, die ich trag im Herzen' and again at 'Sag ihr, über tausend Meilen' resembles sections of the Con moto movement to the Piano Sonata No. 17 D. 850. Much earlier, in *Parole* Op. 7 no. 2, at 'Sie legt das Ohr an den Rasen', Brahms drew very close to Schubert's *Rückblick* from *Die Winterreise* D. 911. Another song from that cycle, *Erstarrung*, is evoked in *Wie rafft' ich mich auf in der Nacht* Op. 32 no. 1. Other references to Schubert may be found in *Wie schnell verschwindet so Licht als Glanz* Op. 33 no. 11, which recalls *Der Atlas* from *Schwanengesang* D. 957 and *Der Neugierige* from *Die schöne Müllerin* D. 795. In *Herbstgefühl* Op. 48 no. 7 the music at 'Im Windhauch schwankt' reminds us of the end of *Der Doppelgänger* (again from *Schwanengesang*) and in *Unbewegte laue Luft* Op. 57 no. 8 the beginning recalls, once more, *Am See* D. 746. Further seemingly direct references, most of them no doubt coincidental, may be found in Brahms's instrumental works, a case being the allusion to the final line of Schubert's *Der Wanderer* D. 463—'Dort, wo du nicht bist, dort ist das Glück'—near the close of his piano Variations Op. 21 no. 1.

It is unwise to assert, as some writings on Brahms's *Lieder* do, that he merely sent his songs off to the publisher when he had a sufficient number finished, assembling his vocal opuses on no other principle. As one whose music was usually so closely argued he would be well aware, for example, of the almost symphonic organization of the keyboard part in Schubert's *Die schöne Müllerin* D. 795 and *Die Winterreise* D. 911 and he would be particularly drawn to the use of contrast in the former cycle. Instances are the manner in which the cheerful brook music of *Wohin?* is opposed to the lullaby of *Des Baches Wiegenlied*; the enquiry of *Dankgesang an den Bach* contrasts with the dialogue of *Der Müller und der Bach*, or how the fresh flowers of *Des Müllers Blumen* have a counterpart in the withered ones of *Trockne Blumen*. Nor would he miss the smaller correspondences, such as the eight minims on the dominant in *Des Baches Wiegenlied* being echoed by eight minims on the dominant at 'Durch den Hain' in *Mein*.

Brahms moved towards a comparable sort of unity, though on a smaller scale, with the two *Junge Lieder* pieces of Op. 63— *Meine Liebe ist grün* and *Wenn um den Hollunder*, and with the three songs called *Heimweh* that conclude the same opus— *Wie traulich war das Fleckchen*, *O wüsst' ich doch den Weg zurück* and *Ich sah als Knabe Blumen blühn*. And whereas in, say, his *Erhebung* Op. 2 no. 3 Schoenberg at the end leaves the voice suspended while the piano seeks a cadence, satisfying closes were not quite so hard to find in Brahms's day and the postludes to *Die Mainacht* Op. 43 no. 2, *Am Sonntag Morgen* Op. 49 no. 1, *Verzagen* Op. 72 no. 4 or *Salamander* Op. 107 no. 2 continue and resolve the mood. Nor did he have any problem in linking, *L'istesso tempo*, *In der Ferne* with its preceding *Scheiden und Meiden* (Op. 19 nos. 3 and 2). Another telling continuation is from *Wiegenlied* to *Abenddämmerung* (Op. 49 nos. 4 and 5), with the latter's expression of adult nostalgia for childhood after the infant goes to sleep.

Such connections have parallels, and on a more specific level, in Brahms's instrumental music, in the way the Adagio mesto of the Horn Trio Op. 40 anticipates the finale theme, and beyond that in the way the last bars of the Andante to his Piano Sonata No. 1 Op. 1 prepare the Scherzo theme (both of

these having precedents in Schumann's Piano Quartet Op.
47). Surely we ought to expect Brahms in his groups of
Lieder to follow the same procedure as in his piano cycles
Opp. 76 and 116–19, each of which is certainly designed to be
played as a whole. He seems in most cases here to have calcu-
lated the exact effect each piece would have following on the
last bars of its predecessor, and the pair of Intermezzos Op. 118
nos. 1 and 2 are an especially good parallel to the songs Op. 49
nos. 4 and 5.

Examples have been given already of sets or even of pairs of
Brahms *Lieder* which should not be separated and also of
groups that do not go well together. To these latter might be
added the nine songs of his Op. 32: their Daumer and Platen
texts unite them at a certain level, yet considerable monotony
results from performing them *en bloc*, especially during the
unmute reproach of Nos. 6, 7 and 8. In most other cases, however, while Brahms's *Lieder* do not often, as he grouped them,
form inviolable structures like Schubert's *Die Winterreise*,
they sometimes follow a perceptible emotional progression, like
Couperin's *Ordres*. The eight songs of Op. 58 are a good example: following the uncommonly extrovert opening of *Blinde
Kuh* and *Während des Regens*, we pass through the mild reproach
of *Die Spröde* and the hope of *O komm, holde Sommernacht*, to the
abrupt despair of *Schwermut*; next the nostalgia for the past of
In der Gasse, is followed by the curious, dreamlike *Vorüber* with
its thoughts of death, and finally the conventional declarations
of *Serenade*, which perhaps mean a new beginning.

In the interpretation of his *Lieder* Brahms greatly valued
spontaneity on a singer's part and for this reason, after about
Op. 19, followed Schubert in adding only a very few expression
marks to the vocal lines. At the same time, as his friend Eduard
Behm tells us (in *Aus meinem Leben*, Berlin, 1911), Brahms
objected quite strongly to diffident performance and sometimes he puts an '*f*' when a '*p*' might have been expected. A
good example is in *Keinen hat es noch gereut*, first of his *Magelone
Romanzen* Op. 33, where at 'Rund um ihn Freuden' he inserts a
poco f although the piano is making a diminuendo to *pp*. A
similar case is *Dein blaues Auge hält so still* Op. 59 no. 8, where
there is an *f* at 'und wie ein See so kühl' although the keyboard

part again has a diminuendo. Such markings in the vocal line at this late date—Op. 59 was published in 1873—are most unusual, however, and more typical is his procedure with the second printing of *Liebestreu* Op. 3 no. 1, for he removed numerous markings that had appeared in the original edition of 1854. Among these were *piano con espressione* at 'O versenk, o versenk', *pianissimo träumerisch* at 'Ein Stein wohl bleibt', *agitato* at 'Und die Treu', together with a considerable variety of accents, staccato dots, etc. Similarly in *Die Liebende schreibt* Op. 47 no. 5 he removed a number of tempo directions from the voice part, but at times he found it hard to make up his mind, changing the tempo marking of *An ein Veilchen* Op. 49 no. 2 from *Un poco allegretto* to *Andante con moto*, and then removing the *con moto*. On occasion Brahms also changed the key of a song at quite a late stage, instances being *Wie bist du, meine Königin* Op. 32 no. 9, which was originally in E (not E flat) major, and *Sonntag* Op. 47 no. 3, which he moved down to G major from A flat which he oddly described in a letter to Simrock as a 'dead' key. It was very unusual for him to change the texture in any way when making these transpositions, but an exception is *Sehnsucht* Op. 49 no. 3, where he altered the accompaniment of the low-voice edition along these lines:

There were also times when he made changes of metre, as in *An ein Veilchen* Op. 49 no. 2, where the alternation between

6/8 and 9/8 at the passage beginning 'O dann schmiege dich ihr ans Herz' was inserted at a late stage, the whole having originally been in 6/8. Again, with *Beim Abschied* Op. 95 no. 3 the whole was first published in 3/8 but in his printed copy Brahms put the accompaniment into 2/4, leaving the vocal line in 3/8, the resultant cross-rhythms certainly adding to the effect of Halm's poem, with its expression of isolation felt amid a crowd of companions.

Particularly with his earliest songs, Brahms sometimes made quite striking changes between the first and subsequent editions. In *Liebe und Frühling* Op. 3 no. 2, for example, he altered the vocal line at bars 5–8 thus:

and the accompaniment in bars 8–11 as follows:

An indecision comparable to that over the tempo marking of *An ein Veilchen* Op. 49 no. 2 was felt in connection with the setting of '*O hört mich, ihr gütigen Sterne/O höre mich grünen die*

Flur', for as initially sent to the publisher the melody stood as it does now; yet Brahms wrote telling him to substitute this considerably different version:

and then again instructing him to reinstate what he had composed in the first place! Another striking melodic revision was made, in the final manuscript copy, to the last four bars of the vocal line to *Sehnsucht* Op. 49 no. 3:

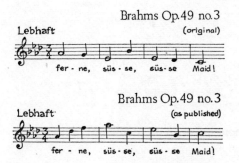

More notable still is the case of *Therese* Op. 86 no. 1, for whose opening line Brahms actually considered this (writing to Elisabet von Herzogenberg for her opinion):

with the following four bars 16–19:

Brahms Op.86 no.1
(proposed revision)

al·le Ratsherrn in der Stadt und al·le Wei·sen der Welt

Brahms Op.86 no.1
(as published)

al·le Ratsherrn in der Stadt und al·le Wei·sen der Welt

Comparing this with the far simpler version eventually published, he said that one was as old as the other, meaning,
presumably, that both alternatives had presented themselves
to him during composition. This in itself is a remarkable
comment on the processes which led finally to the apparent
lyrical spontaneity of his most beautiful melodies. If we think
about it, however, it may just begin to account for their
diversity of expression, for the tenderness of *Minnelied* Op. 71
no. 5, and the nearly inarticulate passion of *Nicht mehr zu dir
zu gehen* Op. 32 no. 2, for the despair of *Der Strom* Op. 32
no. 4 and the light-hearted flirtation of *Vergebliches Ständchen*
Op. 84 no. 4, for the changing moods of *Mädchenfluch* Op. 69
no. 9, the spacious lines of *Erinnerung* Op. 63 no. 2, and the
glowing colours of *Unbewegte laue Luft* Op. 57 no. 8.

Opus
 3 Six Songs (published 1854)
   1 *Liebestreu*
   2 *Liebe und Frühling I*
   3 *Liebe und Frühling II*
   4 *Lied aus dem Gedicht 'Ivan'*
   5 *In der Fremde*
   6 *Lied*

 6 Six Songs (published 1853)
   1 *Spanisches Lied*
   2 *Der Frühling*
   3 *Nachwirkung*
   4 *Juchhe!*
   5 *Wie die Wolke nach der Sonne*
   6 *Nachtigallen schwingen*

 7 Six Songs (published 1854)
   1 *Treue Liebe*
   2 *Parole*
   3 *Anklänge*
   4 *Volkslied*
   5 *Die Trauernde*
   6 *Heimkehr*

 14 Eight Songs and Romances (published 1861)
   1 *Vor dem Fenster*
   2 *Vom verwundeten Knaben*
   3 *Murrays Ermordung*
   4 *Ein Sonett*

5 *So willst du des Armen dich gnädig erbarmen*
6 *Wie soll ich die Freude, die Wonne denn tragen*
7 *War es dir, dem diese Lippen bebten*
8 *Wir müssen uns trennen, geliebtes Saitenspiel*
9 *Ruhe, Süssliebchen*
10 *So tönet denn, schäumende Wellen*
11 *Wie schnell verschwindet so Licht als Glanz*
12 *Muss es eine Trennung geben*
13 *Geliebter, wo zaudert dein irrender Fuss*
14 *Wie froh und frisch mein Sinn sich hebt*
15 *Treue Liebe dauert lange*

43 Four Songs (published 1868)
    1 *Von ewiger Liebe*
    2 *Die Mainacht*
    3 *Ich schell mein Horn ins Jammertal*
    4 *Das Lied vom Herrn von Falkenstein*

46 Four Songs (published 1868)
    1 *Die Kränze*
    2 *Magyarisch*
    3 *Die Schale der Vergessenheit*
    4 *An die Nachtigall*

47 Five Songs (published 1868)
    1 *Botschaft*
    2 *Liebesglut*
    3 *Sonntag*
    4 *O liebliche Wangen*
    5 *Die Liebende schreibt*

48 Seven Songs (published 1868)
    1 *Der Gang zum Liebchen*
    2 *Der Überläufer*
    3 *Liebesklage des Mädchens*
    4 *Gold überwiegt die Liebe*
    5 *Trost in Tränen*
    6 *Vergangen ist mir Glück und Heil*
    7 *Herbstgefühl*

49 Five Songs (published 1868)
  1 *Am Sonntag Morgen*
  2 *An ein Veilchen*
  3 *Sehnsucht*
  4 *Wiegenlied*
  5 *Abenddämmerung*

57 Eight Songs and Ballads (published 1871)
  1 *Von waldbekränzter Höhe*
  2 *Wenn du nur zuweilen lächelst*
  3 *Es träumte mir, ich sei dir teuer*
  4 *Ach, wende diesen Blick*
  5 *In meiner Nächte Sehnen*
  6 *Strahlt zuweilen auch ein mildes Licht*
  7 *Die Schnur, die Perl an Perle*
  8 *Unbewegte laue Luft*

58 Eight Songs and Melodies (published 1871)
  1 *Blinde Kuh*
  2 *Während des Regens*
  3 *Die Spröde*
  4 *O komm, holde Sommernacht*
  5 *Schwermut*
  6 *In der Gasse*
  7 *Vorüber*
  8 *Serenade*

59 Eight Songs and Ballads (published 1873)
  1 *Dämmrung senkte sich von oben*
  2 *Auf dem See*
  3 *Regenlied*
  4 *Nachklang*
  5 *Agnes*
  6 *Eine gute, gute Nacht*
  7 *Mein wundes Herz verlangt nach milder Ruh*
  8 *Dein blaues Auge hält so still*

61 Four Duets for soprano & contralto (published 1874)
  1 *Die Schwestern*
  2 *Klosterfräulein*
  3 *Phänomen*
  4 *Die Boten der Liebe*

63 Nine Songs and Ballads (published 1874)
    1 *Frühlingstrost*
    2 *Erinnerung*
    3 *An ein Bild*
    4 *An die Tauben*
    5 *Junge Lieder I (Meine Liebe ist grün)*
    6 *Junge Lieder II (Wenn um den Hollunder)*
    7 *Heimweh I (Wie traulich war das Fleckchen)*
    8 *Heimweh II (O wüsst' ich doch den Weg zurück)*
    9 *Heimweh III (Ich sah als Knabe Blumen blühn)*

66 Five Duets for soprano & contralto (published 1875)
    1 *Klänge I*
    2 *Klänge II*
    3 *Am Strande*
    4 *Jägerlied*
    5 *Hüt du dich*

69 Nine Songs (published 1877)
    1 *Klage I*
    2 *Klage II*
    3 *Abschied*
    4 *Des Liebsten Schwur*
    5 *Tambourliedchen*
    6 *Vom Strande*
    7 *Über die See*
    8 *Salome*
    9 *Mädchenfluch*

70 Four Songs (published 1877)
    1 *Im Garten am Seegestade*
    2 *Lerchengesang*
    3 *Serenade*
    4 *Abendregen*

71 Five Songs (published 1877)
    1 *Es liebt sich so lieblich im Lenze*
    2 *An den Mond*
    3 *Geheimnis*
    4 *Willst du, dass ich geh?*
    5 *Minnelied*

72 Five Songs (published 1877)
1 *Alte Liebe*
2 *Sommerfäden*
3 *O kühler Wald*
4 *Verzagen*
5 *Unüberwindlich*

75 Four Ballads and Romances for two voices (published 1877)
1 *Edward*
2 *Guter Rat*
3 *So lass uns wandern*
4 *Walpurgisnacht*

84 Five Romances and Songs (published 1882)
1 *Sommerabend*
2 *Der Kranz*
3 *In den Beeren*
4 *Vergebliches Ständchen*
5 *Spannung*

85 Six Songs (published 1882)
1 *Sommerabend*
2 *Mondenschein*
3 *Mädchenlied*
4 *Ade!*
5 *Frühlingslied*
6 *In Waldeseinsamkeit*

86 Six Songs (published 1882)
1 *Therese*
2 *Feldeinsamkeit*
3 *Nachtwandler*
4 *Über die Heide*
5 *Versunken*
6 *Todessehnen*

91 Two Songs with viola obbligato (published 1884)
1 *Gestillte Sehnsucht*
2 *Geistliches Wiegenlied*

94 Five Songs (published 1884)
1 *Mit vierzig Jahren*
2 *Steig auf, geliebter Schatten*
3 *Mein Herz ist schwer*
4 *Sapphische Ode*
5 *Kein Haus, keine Heimat*

95 Seven Songs (published 1884)
1 *Das Mädchen*
2 *Bei dir sind meine Gedanken*
3 *Beim Abschied*
4 *Der Jäger*
5 *Vorschneller Schwur*
6 *Mädchenlied*
7 *Schön war, das ich dir weihte*

96 Four Songs (published 1886)
1 *Der Tod, das ist die kühle Nacht*
2 *Wir wandelten*
3 *Es schauen die Blumen*
4 *Meerfahrt*

97 Six Songs (published 1886)
1 *Nachtigall*
2 *Auf dem Schiffe*
3 *Entführung*
4 *Dort in den Weiden*
5 *Komm bald*
6 *Trennung*

105 Five Songs (published 1889)
1 *Wie Melodien zieht es*
2 *Immer leiser wird mein Schlummer*
3 *Klage*
4 *Auf dem Kirchhofe*
5 *Verrat*

106 Five Songs (published 1889)
1 *Ständchen*
2 *Auf dem See*
3 *Es hing der Reif*

In addition to books mentioned in the text, the following were referred to during the preparation of this work:

BARTH, R. *Brahms und seine Musik* (Hamburg, 1904).

BLUME, W. *Brahms in der Meininger Tradition* (Stuttgart, 1933).

BRAHMS, J. *Briefwechsel* (16 vols.) (Berlin, 1907–22).

CAPELL, R. *Schubert's Songs* (London, 1957).

CLOSS, A. *Genius of the German Lyric* (London, 1961).

DEUTSCH, O. 'First Editions of Brahms' (*Music Review*, 1940).

DIETRICH, A. *Erinnerungen an Brahms in Briefen, besonders aus seiner Jugendzeit* (Leipzig, 1899).

DRINKER, H. *Texts of the Vocal Works of Brahms in English Translation* (New York, 1945).

EHRMANN, A. VON *Brahms—Weg, Werk und Welt* (Leipzig, 1933).

ERNEST, G. *Brahms* (Berlin, 1930).

EVANS, E. (senior) *Historical, Descriptive and Analytical Account of the Entire Works of Brahms*. Vol. I, *The Vocal Works* (London, 1912).

FELLINGER, I. *Über die Dynamik in der Musik von Brahms* (Berlin, 1961).

FISKE, R. 'Brahms and Scotland' (*Musical Times*, 1968).

FOX-STRANGEWAYS, A. 'Brahms's Magelone Romanzen Op. 33' (*Music and Letters*, 1949).

FRIEDLÄNDER, M. *Brahms Lieder, Einführung in seine Gesänge für eine und zwei Stimmen* (Berlin, 1922).

—— *Das Deutsche Lied im 18 Jahrhundert* (Stuttgart, 1902).

—— *Neue Volkslieder von Brahms* (Berlin, 1926).

—— 'Brahms' Volkslieder' (*Peters Jahrbuch*, 1902).

FULLER-MAITLAND, J. *Brahms* (London, 1911).

GAL, H. *Brahms—Werk und Persönlichkeit* (Frankfurt, 1961).

GEIRINGER, K. *Brahms* (London, 1948).

—— 'Brahms as Reader and Collector' (*Musical Quarterly*, 1933).

GEIRINGER, K. 'Brahms als Musikhistoriker' (*Die Musik*, 1933).
—— 'Brahms and Wagner' (*Musical Quarterly*, 1936).
GERBER, R. *Brahms* (Potsdam, 1938).
GOLDMARK, K. *Erinnerungen* (Vienna, 1922).
HADOW, W. *Collected Essays* (Oxford, 1928).
HAMMERMANN, W. *Brahms als Liedkomponist* (Leipzig, 1912).
HENSCHEL, G. *Musings and Memories of a Musician* (London, 1918).
—— 'Recollections of Brahms' (*Royal Institute Proceedings XVIII*, 1906).
HERNRIED, R. *Brahms* (Leipzig, 1934).
HOHENEMSER, R. 'Brahms und die Volksmusik' (*Die Musik*, 1903).
HORTON, J. *Brahms's Orchestral Music* (London, 1969).
HÜBBE, W. *Brahms in Hamburg* (Hamburg, 1902).
HUSCHKE, C. *Brahms als Pianist, Dirigent und Lehrer* (Karlsruhe, 1936).
JENNER, G. *Brahms als Mensch, Lehrer und Künstler* (Marburg, 1905).
JONAS, O. *Das Wesen des musikalischen Kunstwerkes* (Vienna, 1934).
KALBECK, M. *Brahms* (4 vols.) (Berlin, 1904–14).
—— *Brahms als Lyriker* (Vienna, 1921).
KOCH, L. *Brahms in Ungarn* (Budapest, 1933).
KÖHLER, L. *Brahms und seine Stellung in der Musik* (Hanover, 1880).
KOMORN, M. 'Brahms as Choral Conductor' (*Musical Quarterly*, 1933).
KREBS, K. *Des jungen Kreislers Schatzkästlein* (Berlin, 1909).
KROSS, S. *Die Chorwerke von Brahms* (Berlin, 1958).
LAUX, K. *Brahms—Leben und Werk* (Graz, 1944).
LEYEN, R. VON DER *Brahms als Mensch und Freund* (Düsseldorf, 1905).
LIENAU, R. *Erinnerungen an Brahms* (Berlin, 1934).
LITZMANN, B. *Clara Schumann–Johannes Brahms, Briefe 1853–96* (Leipzig, 1927).
MAY, F. *Brahms* (2 vols.) (London, 1905).
MIES, H. *Klaus Groth und die Musik—Erinnerungen an Brahms* (Heide, 1933).
MIES, P. *Stilmomente und Ausdrucksstilformen im Brahms' schen Lied* (Liepzig, 1923).

MIES, P. 'Aus Brahms Werkstatt' (*Simrock Jahrbuch*, 1928).
—— 'Der kritische Rat der Freunde und die Veröffentlichung der Werke bei Brahms' (*Simrock Jahrbuch*, 1929).
MOORE, G. *Singer and Accompanist* (London, 1953).
NAGEL, W. *Brahms* (Stuttgart, 1923).
—— *Brahms als Nachfolger Beethovens* (Stuttgart, 1892).
NEWMAN, E. *Hugo Wolf* (London, 1907).
NIEMANN, W. *Brahms* (Berlin, 1920).
OPHÜLS, G. *Brahms-Texte, Vollständige Sammlung der von Brahms komponierten und musikalisch bearbeiteten Dichtungen* (Berlin, 1897).
—— *Erinnerungen an Brahms* (Berlin, 1921).
PAULI, W. *Brahms* (Berlin, 1907).
PRAWER, S. *German Lyric Poetry* (London, 1952).
—— *Penguin Book of Lieder* (London, 1964).
RIEMANN, H. 'Brahms und die Theorie der Musik' (*Programme Book of the German Brahms Festival*, 1909).
SAMS, E. *Schumann's Songs* (London, 1969).
—— *Wolf's Songs* (London, 1961).
SCHAUFFLER, R. *The Unknown Brahms* (New York, 1933).
SCHERING, A. 'Brahms und seine Stellung in der Musikgeschichte des 19 Jahrhunderts' (*Peters Jahrbuch*, 1932).
SCHRAMM, W. *Brahms in Detmold* (Leipzig, 1933).
SCHUMANN, ELISABETH *German Song* (London, 1948).
SCHUMANN, EUGENIE *Erinnerungen* (Stuttgart, 1927).
SCHWARTZ, H. *Ignaz Brüll und sein Freundeskreis* (Vienna, 1922).
SIMROCK, N. *Thematisches Verzeichnis der bisher im Druck erschienenen Werke von Brahms* (Berlin, 1910).
SPITTA, P. *Brahms* (New York, 1901).
STERN, J. 'Was Goethe Wrong about the German Lied?' (*Publications of the Modern Language Association LXXVII*, 1962).
STEVENS, D. (ed.). *History of Song* (London, 1961).
STURKE, A. *Der Stil in Brahms' Werken* (Würzburg, 1932).
WALKER, A. 'Brahms and Serialism' (*Musical Opinion*, 1958).
WIDMANN, J. *Brahms in Erinnerungen* (Berlin, 1898).
—— *Sizilien und andere Gegenden Italiens* (Frauenfeld, 1912).
WILLIAMS, C. *The Rhythm of Modern Music* (London, 1909).

147